CALIFORNIA CULINARY

Cooking

AT THE ACADEMY

Recipes and Text by Thomas A. Bloom, Ph.D. and Johnathan Robinette, Executive Chef

AS SEEN ON PUBLIC TELEVISION SPONSORED BY

BRAUN

Designed to perform better.

Managing Editor
LINDA BRANDT
,
Assistant Editor
CARL ABBOTT
,
Art Director
BERNIE SCHIMBKE
,
Photographer
NIKOLAY ŽUREK
,
Typographer
NED TAKAHASHI
,
Photo Design
BERNIE SCHIMBKE
,
Food Stylist
AMY McKENZIE
,
Additional Text & Recipe Development
CARL ABBOTT
AMY McKENZIE
,
Print Coordinator
INTERPRINT

Pictured on front cover: Black Pepper Tagliatelle with Spring Vegetable Mélange.

Library of Congress Catalog Number: 91-060965

ISBN: 0-912333-09-X

First Edition

10 9 8 7 6 5 4 3 2

ACKNOWLEDGEMENTS

Many individuals were responsible for bringing COOKING AT THE ACADEMY to fruition.

Thank you to all of the instructors at the Academy who provided professional consultation as well as technical services during the taping of the thirteen half-hour shows and the development of this cookbook: Ian Algerøn, Dan Bowe, Marcel Cathala, David Chomsky, Peter Coulson, Reginald Elgin, Steve Eliot, Bob Fanucchi, Robyn Fisher, Bo Friberg, Marc Halperin, Shelley Handler, Patricia Hart, John Jensen, Jean-Michel Jeudy, Susan Klugerman, Lars Kronmark, Denys Lemay, Brian Mattingly, Jean-Pierre Metivier, Mial Parker, W. Scott Strong, Greg Tompkins, Rosina Wilson, Donald Woods and Rhoda Yee.

Thanks to the spouses and family members of the California Culinary Academy faculty for their patience, understanding and tolerance during the three months of taping.

Thanks to all of the students at the Academy who demonstrated understanding and patience. Your encouragement and motivation were an inspiration to the faculty and staff. A special thanks to Carl Abbott and to the externship students Tom Anderson, Julio Hawkins and Jeff Moschetti who spent countless hours in the kitchen providing the necessary backup to make each show a culinary success.

Thanks also to Linda Carucci, Dean of the Academy; Sally Sacchetto, Vice President of Operations; Lloyd Hickey, Purchasing Manager; and all of their staff whose behind-the-scenes participation and efforts made for a smooth transition between operating each day as a professional school and a television studio.

Working on this series with a professional such as Johnathan Robinette, Executive Chef of the California Culinary Academy, was one of the great pleasures in life for me. His high standards and commitment to excellence, as well as his philosophy of cooking are evidenced in each of the shows as well as in this companion cookbook.

Executive Administrative Assistant, Amanda Galaup, has been a talented organizer, administrator and scheduling director who always manages to meet unreasonable deadlines with a smile and professional results. How fortunate I am to have her as part of the Academy family.

Special thanks to Marjorie Poore, Vice President, National Productions; gayle yamada, Executive Producer; Bruce Franchini, Producer; and Donna Homer, Director of Marketing who once again demonstrated why KQED is the nation's leading public television producer of cooking programs.

Thanks to the generosity of Ellyn Luros, President of Computrition in Chatsworth, California, for providing the nutritional analysis in the cookbook.

Finally, a special thank you to Braun Inc. and to Alex McKinnon, Braun's Product Manager for the underwriting of the series, COOKING AT THE ACADEMY.

Thomas A. Bloom, Ph.D.
President and CEO
The California Culinary Academy

TABLE OF CONTENTS

PRODUCER'S THANKS

The success of making a television series depends on a harmonious collaboration of many different but compatible talents. There are no individual "stars"—it is a team effort, an ensemble performance.

The production team is the heart of a television series, and I am indeed fortunate to have been able to work with such a dedicated group of people. They are the men and women whose names go racing past your television screen, often at break-neck and unreadable speed, in the last few seconds of each program. They are the ones who worked many days at a stretch over long, often impossible hours no sane person would choose if he/she had a choice—and did it with unsurpassed grace, understanding and professionalism. Without them, COOKING AT THE ACADEMY would simply not exist, and I am especially happy to acknowledge further their contributions here.

To Coordinating Producer Jamie Stobie for her great attention to detail; to Associate Producers Linda Brandt and June Ouellette who are, quite simply, the best; to our Unit Manager, the unflappable Jolee Hoyt for her calm handling of those of us whose "flap-factor" was too often gargantuan; to Technical Director Dick Schiller; to Wes Dorman and Vaughn Kilgore who so beautifully photographed the series; to Lighting Director Mike Van Dine and his assistants Cliff Henry and Chris Furbee; to Margaret Clarke and Jim Summers, our Floor Directors, who were our "jacks-of-all-trades" and masters as well; to our Audio Assistants Fred Tetzner, Gary Gerwig, Kevin Cates and Rick Ratusz who helped to capture every chop and sizzle; to our Off-Line Editors Kitty Rea, Jon Herbst and Terry Kane Chinn who crafted each program into a cohesive unit; and to our On-Line Editors John Andreini, Dick Schiller, Helen Silvani, Bill Swan, Bob Sweeney and Fred Meyers who put the icing on the cake; to John Clairbourne, Eric Shackelford, Frederick Perry, Tomas Tucker and Jerry Jarocki for their contributions to the opening and closing sequences; to djovida, Dovel Devon and Jim Raeside for post-production audio; to Jan Black and Matt Elmore our announcers; to Operations Production Managers John Parola and Eric Dauster; to Larry Reid and Jim MacIllvaine for their constant support; to Jon Herbst for composing and performing the music for COOKING AT THE ACADEMY; to our Designer Alan Voorhees and Publicists Cynthia Traina and Charlotte Knabel; and to our production interns Roshinee Punian, Simone Nittel, Jim Hollander and Jane Schneider.

A special thank you to Marjorie Poore, Vice President, National Productions and to Executive Producer, gayle k. yamada with whom work is always a special joy.

Last, but not least, to the people of the California Culinary Academy—the chef/instructors, administration and students who have been acknowledged by Dr. Thomas A. Bloom on page 3, and to Chefs Ralph Bürgin and Dan Mullin for their special assistance.

My heartfelt thanks and gratitude to you all.

Bruce Franchini, Producer
COOKING AT THE ACADEMY

INTRODUCTION

Evidenced by the increase of speciality food stores, gourmet sections of grocery stores, food magazines, cookbooks, cooking classes and professional chef training schools, we have witnessed a tremendous growth in the interest of food and cooking throughout the world.

COOKING AT THE ACADEMY was written for the home cook who is interested in learning basic techniques. These techniques include: poaching and steaming; grilling and broiling; sautéing; frying; braising and stewing; and roasting and baking.

The basic philosophy of the television series COOKING AT THE ACADEMY and this companion cookbook is to teach the fundamental cooking techniques that are the foundations of all cuisines, and to introduce the viewer to the herbs, spices and flavoring agents unique to the many cuisines of the world.

The recipes developed for the television show COOKING AT THE ACADEMY and the additional recipes presented in this cookbook include salt, butter, eggs and cream, but focus on moderation and balance as opposed to elimination. The great chefs of today have not abandoned the use of these ingredients in their cooking, but instead have reduced their dependence on them and have focused on incorporating herbs, spices and flavoring agents to add flavor, color and texture to their food.

The information and recipes presented in this book reflect the expertise of the professional chef/instructors of the California Culinary Academy and will serve as an excellent resource for both the novice and the experienced cook.

Enjoy!

Thomas A. Bloom, Ph.D.

KNOWING THE BASICS

TECHNIQUES

BLANCHING

Blanching, poaching and steaming are similar cooking techniques because each involves cooking food in or around water. Blanching refers to a light cooking of raw ingredients, most often in boiling water. Some ingredients are blanched in boiling water, then shocked in ice water to preserve crunch and color.

Although blanching and refreshing vegetables in large amounts of boiling water is common in many restaurant kitchens, cooks are beginning to acknowledge that this is not the most effective technique for preserving nutrients. Many cooks now recommend blanching in small amounts of water, just until the water disappears, thus retaining the maximum amount of vitamins and minerals.

Blanching intensifies the color of vegetables. Green vegetables, or those which contain chlorophyll as their primary pigment, are sensitive to acids. Acids, like lemon juice or vinegar, turn green vegetables yellow during blanching. To enhance the color, add a pinch of an alkaline (salt or baking soda) to the blanching water.

Other vegetables, like cauliflower, onions, white cabbage and parsnips, are sensitive to alkaline. To retain their whiteness, add a few drops of lemon juice or vinegar to the blanching water.

POACHING

Poaching is different from blanching in several ways: (1) the food is cooked longer, (2) the temperature of the poaching liquid is no more than 160° to 180°F and (3) the poaching liquid is often well seasoned.

TECHNIQUES

Court bouillon is a spiced, aromatic liquid that is used to poach fish and other foods. In addition to water, it contains an acid like lemon, tomato or vinegar, a stock and aromatic vegetables and spices.

STEAMING

Steaming is a very gentle cooking technique and is differentiated from blanching or poaching in that the food sits above the water rather than directly in it. Since foods are not placed in water, steamed foods tend to retain their water soluble nutrients as well as most of the delicate flavors.

At sea level, steam is created at the same temperature that water boils (212°F) and therefore is considered a low-temperature cooking technique. Steaming neither changes the color of food nor enriches its flavor and because steam is created at a relatively low temperature, the process can be long when steaming dense-textured food. For that reason, you can shorten the cooking time by cutting food into smaller pieces.

A common way to steam is to fill a pot one-fourth full of liquid, usually water, then suspend a grid or perforated rack just above it. The liquid should be replenished as needed. It is important to cover the pan tightly when steaming and not to remove it until the end of cooking.

By definition, steaming can also take place in the oven. Cooking in parchment paper, such as with a piece of fish layered with herbs and vegetables, is also considered steaming because the fish steams in its own juices until cooked.

TECHNIQUES

GRILLING/BROILING

Both grilling and broiling make use of intense direct (or indirect) heat. In grilling, food cooks on a grid over heat that is produced by a burning material or heating element. In broiling, the heat source, either a gas flame or electric element, comes from above. Both techniques are considered healthy cooking methods, especially with meat, because the internal fats of the meat tend to drip away.

In restaurant kitchens, a wood-burning, gas or electric grill is common. A restaurant broiler, called a *salamander,* is a separate unit usually suspended from the ceiling of the kitchen at eye level.

In home kitchens with a proper ventilation system, grilling has become a popular option. Either a gas or electric grill, which makes use of lava rocks or synthetic briquettes, can be recessed down into the cabinet so that it is flush with the surrounding countertop. The ventilation system consists of a hood or large exhaust system and is usually positioned directly over the grill/ stovetop area. It is capable of removing large amounts of smoke from the cooking area.

Outdoor grilling remains a popular alternative to broiling in an oven indoors. Grills, ranging from small hibachi-type open grills to large, round or rectangular covered barbecues, make use of many different kinds of fuels such as charcoal briquettes, mesquite or hardwood charcoal, natural gas or propane.

For adding a unique flavor to grilled foods, you can supplement traditional cooking fuels with pre-soaked chunks of natural wood such as Hickory, Alder or wood from fruit trees. Fresh herbs and fruit rinds also can be added to burning fuels. Some choices are: fresh thyme, bay, oregano, marjoram, or rosemary as well as lemon, orange or lime rinds, or fresh sliced ginger. All of these suggestions work best on a covered grill. Simply moisten the herbs/rinds and toss them on the burning coals just before adding the food.

TECHNIQUES

Tips for Grilling:

(1) Make sure that the grill (or broiler) is thoroughly clean and hot before cooking.

(2) To prevent food from sticking, either lightly brush the grill with a heat-resistant oil before grilling or brush the food prior to cooking.

(3) Close the top of the grill to enhance a smoky flavor.

SAUTEING

Sautéing is a cooking process where ingredients are quickly cooked over moderate to high heat in a small amount of fat in a large, flat-bottomed pan. The word "sauté" comes from the French word *sauter* – a verb meaning to jump. The technique is so named because a cook does not stir when sautéing food. While the pan is on the burner, the cook pulls it toward him/her with a rapid jerk. The food catches on the far lip of the pan, causing the food to "jump" in the air, thus rearranging the food without stirring.

Because sautéing is a high-heat method of cooking, the fat used in the pan should not be one that burns easily. Fats that contain other solids will burn quickly. Examples are butter, which contains milk solids, extra virgin olive oil, which contains olive solids, and nut oils, which contain nut solids. Fats that are heat resistant include most vegetable oils, corn oil, safflower oil, pure olive oil and canola oil.

After food is sautéed, a glaze often forms in the bottom of the pan caused by high heat that crystallized the sugars and juices in the food. This very concentrated glaze is used by the cook in a process called *deglazing*. When deglazing, the cook pours a room-temperature liquid, such as wine or stock, into the hot sauté pan and scrapes loose the brown particles from the bottom of the pan creating a flavorful base for the sauce.

TECHNIQUES

Tips for Sautéing:

(1) Be sure that the items to be sautéed are cut into uniform pieces. This will ensure uniform cooking time.

(2) Dry off raw ingredients before adding to the sauté pan so that they do not splatter hot oil.

(3) Select a pan that is large enough to allow all foods to move freely. A crowded sauté pan will result in steamed, rather than sautéed food. If no glaze forms, there is too much liquid in the pan.

(4) Use a small amount of heat-resistant fat for sautéing.

(5) Heat pan and fat very well prior to adding any raw ingredients. This shortens cooking time and eliminates unnecessary absorption of oil.

FRYING

Frying is identified as cooking in hot fat. By definition, both stir-frying and sautéing could be considered frying but in today's cooking, we refer to fried foods as those which are cooked in substantial amounts of fat. We further define frying as a cooking technique in which at least one-half of the food is submerged in fat.

Two types of frying are suggested in this cookbook: deep-frying and pan-frying. Deep-fried foods, which are often coated with a batter before frying, are totally submerged in hot fat whereas in pan-frying, food is only half submerged and usually has a flour or crumb coating. Common deep-fried items are French fried potatoes and onion rings, fried fish, fritters and tempura. All of these items call for a batter, which not only adds extra flavor to the food but also adds a delicate crispness.

It is important to test the temperature of the oil before frying. Drop a small piece of bread into the oil. If it sinks, the oil is not hot

TECHNIQUES

enough. If it stays at the top and browns immediately, the oil is probably too hot. But if the bread sinks slightly, then comes back to the surface and begins to brown, the temperature is perfect. Pan-fried foods, such as fried chicken, are usually given a coating of crumbs or flour before frying. The pan, which should be heavy enough to distribute the heat evenly, is partially filled with oil. When the oil becomes hot, the food is added. Pan-fried foods need to be turned over during cooking. Because both types of frying involve relatively high heat, usually between 325° and 360°F, choose oils for frying such as canola oil, corn oil, vegetable oil or pure olive oil, as they withstand higher temperatures.

Tips for Frying:

(1)   Use heavy pans to distribute the heat evenly.

(2)   Use oil for frying such as canola, corn, vegetable or pure olive oil because they are able to withstand high temperatures.

(3)   Test the oil temperature, making sure that it is hot before adding raw ingredients.

(4)   Use caution when cooking with hot oil. Spills can be very dangerous because oil tends to retain heat even when spread out thinly. Remember that oil and grease fires are not extinguished with water. Small fires can be smothered by cutting off the source of oxygen, such as by covering the pan with another pan. It's a good idea to keep a small kitchen fire extinguisher handy, as well.

BRAISING / STEWING

Braising is a low-heat cooking technique in which food is cooked in a small amount of liquid in a closed container for a long time. Ideal for large cuts of tough meat and for vegetables that must be cooked thoroughly, braising can also be used for cooking certain fish–those with firm texture which hold up to long cooking times.

TECHNIQUES

Braising helps to make tough meat tender by breaking down both kinds of connective tissue, collagen and elastin. Collagen, which is white and turns to gelatin and water when exposed to moist heat, can also be tenderized by the addition of an acid, such as wine or tomatoes, or other acidic ingredients placed in the braising liquid.

Foods are most often browned before braising. Browning caramelizes any outside sugars, thus intensifying flavor, and helps to seal in the juices. After the braising liquid is added and the food is slowly cooked over a period of time, a rich liquid develops which is often reduced and used as the sauce.

The liquid added when braising food varies with the type of ingredients used. Red meats often call for beef or veal stock, or red wine, while poultry may call for vegetable or chicken stock, or white wine.

The braising pan is usually oval or rectangular and fairly deep. A tight-fitting lid is a must and solid handles make removing the pan from the oven much easier. Most are made of copper, aluminum or cast iron; however, clay pots, which have been fired for heat resistance, can be used for braising, too.

Tips for Braising:

(1)   Select a braising pot with a tight-fitting lid.

(2)   For a richer flavor, brown meat before braising.

(3)   When braising, add a small amount of liquid in the beginning, then replenish during cooking. Large amounts of liquids tend to boil foods and dilute their flavor.

(4)   Slice braised meats thinly across the grain, to serve.

TECHNIQUES

ROASTING

Roasting and baking are similar cooking techniques, relying on the use of radiant heat in an oven. Spit-roasting, the original roasting method, was used primarily to cook meats, fish and fowl. Meat was skewered onto a large pole, then turned slowly over the open fire until roasted through. Oven roasting, the technique most used today, is done in a hot oven with the food resting in a pan on the oven rack. Food is sometimes seared on top of the stove, then allowed to roast until the proper internal temperature is reached.

Roasting food has its advantages. Because high heat is used, foods tend to caramelize, thus producing a beautiful rich brown color and a complex, well-developed flavor. Roasting food also tends to require less attention than other types of cooking, such as sautéing.

For roasted vegetables, the doneness check is poking with a fork to determine the degree of tenderness. Food should be allowed to rest after it has roasted to allow the tissues to relax and the juices to stabilize.

BAKING

Baking, which uses a lower oven temperature than roasting, is used for gentle cooking of easily scorched foods, primarily those containing flour.

The evenness of the heat in the oven is crucial to baking. Often ovens that are used specifically for baking are equipped with stone or brick floors to collect and to evenly distribute the heat. These ovens are also equipped with a mechanism that allows steam to enter at controlled intervals, for a controlled amount of time. This steam feature can be duplicated in home ovens by spraying cool water into the oven and quickly shutting the door or by placing a pan of water on a rack below the baking item.

TECHNIQUES

If your oven has hot spots–places which cook faster than others–you can avoid burning by changing the position of the food in the oven often and by using thicker or double-ply baking pans. To ensure even baking of cookies, simply invert an empty cookie sheet and place on the oven rack. Place the filled cookie sheet on top, thus guaranteeing that the bottom of the cookie sheet will be evenly heated.

Convection ovens, which circulate heat evenly by the use of a fan, are advantageous for baking delicate items.

GLOSSARY

Ingredients and techniques are fundamental to cooking and every cook, whether a culinary novice or experienced professional, can benefit from knowledge gained by simply reading a well-written cookbook.

The following glossary is a list of basic cooking terms–words used to describe ingredients, methods of cooking, utensils and tests for doneness that are unique to a particular type of food. The terminology is easy to understand and can be applied to any recipe.

As a point of reference, all of the italicized words in the recipe instructions appear in alphabetical order in the glossary. The majority of the entries deal with ingredients and processes used in everyday cooking. For example, in many recipes we refer to "deglazing a pan" with wine or stock, or to making a "roux" using butter and flour. The glossary offers a concise explanation of those terms. Likewise, when a candy recipe refers to the "hard-crack stage" or a certain consistency or temperature, you will know what to look for if you scan through the following pages first!

Our abbreviated glossary is in no way a complete compilation of food terms but it should familiarize the reader with the various cooking terms, techniques, ingredients and utensils called for in COOKING AT THE ACADEMY.

GLOSSARY

Al Dente Italian phrase meaning "to the tooth." Used as a test for doneness for vegetables or pasta; implies slightly firm, not soft or mushy.

Ancho Chile Powder Dark, reddish-brown chile powder made from dried Poblano chili peppers, a variety of *Capsicum longum*, a regional pepper grown in the Southwest. Intensity and flavor range from mild to very pungent. Should be used sparingly.

Arrowroot A fine white powder or starch, extracted from a tropical rhizome or underground root, that is used to thicken sauces and soups. Because of its clarity, appearance and the absence of any taste of its own, it is considered superior to cornstarch as an all-purpose thickening agent.

Au Gratin Having a browned or crusted top made from fine bread crumbs that is usually placed under the broiler. Often implies the use of grated or shredded cheese, and/or a rich sauce or combination of ingredients that are served in the dish in which they are cooked.

Au Jus Pan drippings or natural juices. An accompaniment made by straining juices from a roasting pan and served without thickening.

Au Sec To cook "until dry."

Bain-Marie A bain-marie or "water bath" is a container placed inside of (or over) a second container filled with hot water. It is used to gently cook food by surrounding it with simmering water.

Bake A dry-heat process of cooking where a raw ingredient is surrounded by hot air in a closed oven. The air contains some moisture that has been released from the food being baked. The term usually applies to breads, pastries, vegetables and fish.

Balsamic Vinegar A barrel-aged vinegar, dark in color with a mellow, sweet/sour character, made from the *Trebbiano* grape in the region surrounding Modena, Italy.

Ballotine A hot or cold dish, usually made with boneless poultry, meat or fish, that has been stuffed, rolled and trussed before cooking. Usually a ballotine is roasted, poached or braised.

GLOSSARY

Basmati Rice A distinctively-flavored, aromatic variety of long grain rice, very small in size, that originates from India or Pakistan.

Bâtonnet Usually a descriptive term for a vegetable cut into small sticks or "batons," approximately ¼-inch by ¼-inch by 2 or 3 inches long.

Béarnaise A classical emulsion sauce (similar to hollandaise) made by combining egg yolks and a reduction of white wine, vinegar, shallots and tarragon, whisked together over low heat with the addition of butter and finished with chervil.

Béchamel A simple sauce made by combining a light *roux* (butter and flour cooked to a paste consistency) and milk. Béchamel is the basis of other sauces. With the addition of crayfish it becomes Nantua, with Gruyère cheese it becomes Mornay and with onions it becomes Soubise.

Beurre Manié A smooth paste, made from equal parts of butter and flour, used to thicken sauces. Usually whisked into a boiling liquid, a few small pieces at a time, until well blended.

Beurre Noisette Butter that has been gently heated in a sauté pan until it gives off a nutty-like aroma and turns golden brown in color. Often called "hazelnut butter" or "brown butter."

Bisque A thick, rich soup made with a crustacean or vegetable purée, classically thickened with rice and finished with cream.

Blanch A cooking technique where a raw ingredient is partially cooked for a brief period of time in boiling water or in hot fat. As in a preparation technique, blanching tends to set colors, loosen skins and peels, while sealing flavors.

Boil A cooking technique where a raw ingredient is cooked in water (or other liquid) that is bubbling rapidly, as well as maintaining a constant temperature of 212°F.

GLOSSARY

Bombe A layered, molded ice cream or frozen dessert, usually a half-sphere in shape, that is often decorated with whipped cream, nuts and/or candied fruit.

Braise A cooking technique where a raw ingredient is usually seared in fat and then tightly covered and cooked, partially-submerged in a small amount of liquid, over low heat for a long period of time.

Broil A cooking technique where a raw ingredient is cooked with radiant heat from above, usually with a gas flame or an electric element.

Brunoise Items cut to a small dice, approximately ⅛-inch by ⅛-inch by ⅛-inch. When vegetables are cut in this manner, they are usually used as a garnish. A *fine brunoise* is cut into ¹⁄₁₆-inch by ¹⁄₁₆-inch by ¹⁄₁₆-inch.

Buttercream A light and creamy uncooked icing made from butter blended with confectioner's sugar (or sugar syrup) and eggs. Occasionally a small amount of flavoring is added as well a small amount of margarine or shortening for stabilization.

Canola Oil Light, neutral tasting oil containing 5% saturated fatty acids, 15% mono-saturated and 15% polyunsaturated fat. Also called *rape-seed oil* or *colza oil.* Best usage is in low-temperature cooking.

Caramelization The browning of natural sugars. This occurs between 320° and 360°F.

Chiffonade A preparation technique where leafy greens, such a fresh herbs or lettuce, are cut into thin strips or shreds of varying thickness.

China Cap A cone-shaped, fine meshed strainer with a handle, usually made out of metal, that allows liquid to pass through. Used for straining and puréeing foods. Also called a *chinois.*

Chowder A thick, hearty soup, made from a variety of ingredients, usually thickened with potatoes.

GLOSSARY

Clarified Butter Butter from which the milk solids and water have been removed leaving pure butterfat. Clarified butter has a higher smoking point but less of a butter flavor.

Compound Butter A mixture of raw butter and various flavoring ingredients, such as minced herbs, lemon zest, or spices, creamed to a smooth consistency.

Concassée Something that has been coarsely chopped; most common usage is to describe skinless, seeded tomatoes.

Consommé Rich, flavorful concentrated broth that has been clarified to make it clear and transparent.

Cornet Tiny, conical piping bag, shaped from a triangular piece of parchment or waxed paper, used for piping precise or delicate decorations.

Couverture Descriptive term for a type of light or dark chocolate with increased cocoa butter content. Primary usage is for coating and decorating. Couverture-quality chocolate contains between 31% to 38% cocoa butter.

Crème Fraîche Cream to which a cultured bacteria has been added, thus creating a slightly tangy flavor. To make crème fraîche, combine ¼ cup unflavored yogurt (or sour cream) with 2 cups of heavy cream. Cover with cheesecloth and allow to stand at room temperature for about 24 hours.

Creole Sauce A variation of Basic Tomato Sauce, flavored with garlic, onion, green pepper, cayenne pepper, bay leaf and other seasonings.

Cumberland Sauce Tangy cold sauce made with red currant jelly, Port wine, citrus juices and zest, and dry mustard.

Deep-Fry A cooking technique where a raw ingredient, usually coated with bread crumbs or batter, is submerged and cooked in hot fat.

Deglaze To swirl a small amount of liquid in a pan at moderate heat to dissolve cooked particles or caramelized drippings remaining on the bottom of a pan after sautéing or roasting.

GLOSSARY

Demi-glace A rich brown sauce, made from equal portions of Brown Stock and Brown Sauce, that has been reduced. Often used as a concentrated base for other sauces.

Egg Wash A mixture of eggs (yolks and/or whites) beaten with a pinch of salt and generally thinned with water or milk. Used to give shine to baked items or as an adhesive, such as when sealing the edges of ravioli together.

Emulsion A uniform mixture of two non-mixable liquids (usually oil and water) in which one is suspended within the other. Emulsions may be stabilized with an egg or mustard and are classified as temporary, semi-permanent or permanent.

Espagñole (see Sauce Espagñole)

Forcemeat A seasoned mixture of chopped or finely minced ingredients used as a filling, such as in pâté or sausage-making. Also called *farce* or stuffing.

Fry A cooking technique where a raw ingredient is cooked in hot fat over moderate heat.

Ganache A smooth mixture of dark or light chocolate, butter and cream used for filling sweets, glazing or a basis for candy, such as with truffles.

Gazpacho A cold Spanish soup, traditionally made from chopped or puréed raw vegetables.

Glaze To give an item a shiny surface by brushing it with an icing, sauce or an aspic. For meat, to coat with a sauce and brown it in an oven.

Grill A cooking technique where a raw ingredient is placed on an open grid over a radiant heat source.

Guides See Perimeter Bars.

GLOSSARY

Hard-crack Stage A condition registering 300° to 310°F on a candy thermometer, in which a drop of boiling sugar syrup shatters into hard, brittle threads when immersed in cold water.

Hollandaise One of the five primary sauces. A classic emulsion sauce made from a vinegar reduction, clarified butter and egg yolks, flavored with lemon juice.

Hungarian Sauce A variation of Velouté Sauce to which a reduction of white wine, onions and paprika has been added.

Infused Oil A seasoned oil made by combining a light oil with a flavoring agent, such as blanched, puréed herbs or spices, sometimes done over heat.

Italian Meringue A dense, hot meringue made by gradually pouring a boiling sugar syrup (250°F) slowly into partially-beaten egg whites, which is then beaten to a stiff peak consistency.

Julienne A preparation technique where an ingredient is cut into very thin sticks approximately ⅛-inch by ⅛-inch by 1 to 2 inches long. Usually a descriptive term for vegetables.

Macerate The act of soaking a food (generally fruits) in a liquid to incorporate the flavors.

Mandoline A folding, manually operated kitchen tool with numerous adjustable blades designed for slicing.

Marinate A preparation technique where a food is soaked in a seasoned liquid, powder or paste, usually for the purpose flavoring and/or tenderizing.

Marsala A rich slightly smokey flavored, sweet to semi-dry wine from Sicily.

Mayonnaise A cold emulsion sauce made from oil and vinegar emulsified with egg yolk. Considered one of two leading cold sauces.

Mélange A selected blend, mixture or combination of ingredients.

GLOSSARY

Melon Baller A small hand tool whose curved, cup-shaped blade is used for cutting fruits, vegetables and other soft-fleshed foods into balls. Also called a "Parisienne scoop."

Mince A preparation technique where an ingredient is chopped into very fine pieces.

Mirepoix A mixture of roughly-cut or evenly-diced, aromatic vegetables, herbs and spices used for flavoring stock, soups, and stews. A basic vegetable mirepoix contains fifty percent onion, twenty-five percent carrot and and twenty-five percent celery.

Mise en Place French term meaning "put in place." The setup and preparation that is done before beginning a recipe. This includes the ingredients, tools, equipment and serving pieces.

Panade (a) A paste, usually made by combining bread, eggs and cream, that is used to thicken and bind forcemeats in a pâté or sausage.

Pan-Fry A cooking technique where a raw ingredient is cooked over moderate heat in a liberal amount of fat in an uncovered pan.

Parchment Paper Non-waxed, moisture and heat-resistant baking paper, sold in sheets or rolls, that is used for many culinary purposes. Examples are: cooking in parchment (*en papillote*), making small piping bags, and lining baking sheets.

Pastry Bag Soft, pliable canvas, plastic or nylon bag opened at both ends, often sold with a selection of numbered plain or star-shaped metal tips, used to pipe fillings, puréed foods or icings.

(en) Papillote A preparation technique where raw ingredients are wrapped in paper (or aluminum foil) and then cooked, causing the food to steam in its own moisture.

GLOSSARY

Perimeter Bars A set of solid aluminum bars, often used as two sets of matching pairs, used in a number of ways in candy and dessert making.

Philadelphia-style Ice Cream An uncooked ice cream usually made without eggs. Slightly grainier than custard-based ice creams.

Poach A technique where raw ingredients are cooked very gently in simmering water or other liquid (about 160° to 180°F).

Portuguese A variation of Basic Tomato Sauce made by adding onions, tomato concassée, garlic and parsley.

Primary (Mother) Sauces The five basic sauces, most often used in the production of secondary sauces. The primary sauces include: Béchamel, Velouté, Brown Sauce/Sauce Espagñole, Tomato Sauce and Hollandaise.

Purée A preparation technique in which a food has been finely mashed and/or strained to a thick, smooth pulp-like consistency. Name used to describe food prepared in this manner.

Reduce A cooking technique where a liquid is boiled rapidly until the quantity is decreased to a desired consistency by evaporation, thus concentrating the flavor.

Relish A well-seasoned mixture of chopped vegetables and/or fruits, often preserved with sugar and/or vinegar, used as an accompaniment or garnish to offer contrast of flavors and texture to a plate.

Ribbon Stage Describes a stage where ingredients–typically eggs and sugar– have been beaten together to a certain consistency. A mixture is thick, pale yellow in color and forms a ribbon-like design when it is lifted and allowed to fall back into the bowl.

GLOSSARY

Roast A cooking technique where a raw ingredient is cooked surrounded by hot, dry air in an oven or on a spit over an open fire.

Roux A paste-like mixture of equal parts of flour and a fat (usually butter) cooked to varying stages and used to thicken liquids. The length of cooking time determines the color and flavor of the roux. Roux are white, pale blonde or brown. A light roux is used for making light soups as well as for cream and white sauces, while a dark roux is used for making dark-colored soups and heavier sauces.

Sachet A bag of spices and aromatic fresh herbs, tied together in a cheesecloth bundle, that is used for flavoring a stock or sauce. A typical sachet contains parsley stems, cracked peppercorns, dried thyme and a bay leaf.

Sauce Espagñole One of the five primary sauces, most often used in the production of secondary sauces. Made by combining a brown stock, a brown roux, caramelized mirepoix and tomato paste (or purée) and other seasonings.

Sauce Verte Mayonnaise-based sauce mixed with a purée of blanched herbs (parsley, chervil and tarragon) and puréed spinach and/or watercress.

Sauté A cooking technique where raw ingredients are quickly cooked in a small amount of fat in a large, flat-bottomed pan. Comes from the French word *sauter,* meaning "to jump." In sautéing, the pan is pulled toward you with a rapid jerk motion. The food catches on the far lip of the pan, causing the food to "jump" in the air and rearrange in the pan.

Scald A cooking technique where liquid is heated to just below the boiling point (180°-190°F).

Semolina Hard durum wheat ground into granules and made into coarsely ground flour. Unlike flour, when cooked semolina retains its texture.

Simmer A cooking technique where a raw ingredient is cooked in water (or other liquid) over low heat while bubbling slowly, as well as maintaining a temperature (about 185°F) just below boiling.

GLOSSARY

Simple Syrup A sugar syrup made by combining water, granulated sugar and light corn syrup, cooked over low heat until clear and then boiled until desired concentration is reached.

Soft-ball Stage A condition registering 234° to 240°F on a candy thermometer, in which a drop of boiling sugar syrup forms soft, pliable ball when immersed in cold water.

Soft-crack Stage A condition registering 270° to 290° F on a candy thermometer, in which a drop of boiling sugar syrup forms firm, pliable threads when immersed in cold water.

Sorbet (Sherbet) A frozen flavored ice, usually made from fruit juice and/or purée, that is similar to ice cream but does not contain any fat or egg yolk.

Spanish Sauce A variation of Basic Tomato Sauce made by adding onions, tomato concassée, garlic and parsley.

Steam A cooking technique where raw ingredients are cooked directly or indirectly by the steam created from boiling water or other liquids. Perhaps the best method of retaining a food's natural texture, shape, flavor, and vitamin and mineral content.

Stew A cooking technique, similar to braising, where raw ingredients are browned, covered with a liquid and then simmered.

Suprême Sauce A variation of Velouté Sauce. Made by reducing the velouté by one-fourth, adding cream, half-and-half or milk and then finishing with the addition of butter.

Sweat A cooking technique where a raw ingredient is cooked in a small amount of fat over low to medium heat without caramelization/color until it softens and releases moisture.

GLOSSARY

Temper A technique where two ingredients, each with different temperatures are successfully combined. By adding small amounts of the hotter ingredient to the cooler one, you begin to balance their temperatures before folding them together.

Terrine A loaf of forcemeat or vegetables similar to a pâté, cooked in a covered mold (sometimes called a *terrine*) in a bain-marie.

Tourner (Tourné) A trimmed and shaped vegetable or fruit, cut with a *tourné* or turning knife, in a variety of uniformed shapes, thus guaranteeing a similar cooking time.

Velouté Sauce One of the five primary sauces, most often used in the production of secondary sauces. Made by thickening a light-colored stock with a light roux.

Zest The colored and fragrant outer portion of citrus rind.

Zester Small hand tool used for removing the colored portion of citrus peel in thin strips.

A WORD ABOUT STOCK

A knowledgeable chef once defined a good stock as "the aromatic, flavorful source from which the essential character of all cuisine is created." In simple terms, a good stock can make the difference between a mediocre meal and one of distinction.

When it comes to choosing ingredients, consider stock-making the exception to the rule since young and tender ingredients are not necessary. To the contrary, mature more flavorful meat and vegetables are particularly desired when making a stock. (Of course, discretion is still the watchword—the use of very old or inferior ingredients will result in a flavorless stock.)

White stocks are made with light-colored meats, such as veal bones and poultry carcasses, as well as herbs and diced aromatic vegetables known as *mirepoix*. Brown stocks, although containing similar herbs and a mirepoix, are made with beef, veal and poultry bones that have been roasted prior to use.

Essential to the preparation of a good-quality stock is the extraction of rich, intense flavors achieved by long, slow cooking. Since pure, clean flavors are desired in any stock, it is important to skim the foamy, albuminous impurities from the surface to prevent cloudiness and bitterness. Skim the surface once in the first few minutes of cooking, then occasionally thereafter as the stock continues to simmer.

Cooking times will vary. Lighter, more delicate stocks, such as Basic Vegetable Stock (page 30) and Basic Fish Stock (page 32), cook in a shorter period of time than their heavier counterparts, Basic Chicken Stock (page 31) and Basic Beef Stock (page 33).

Seasonings should be used sparingly. Taste your stock often and pay particular attention to the use of salt which tends to intensify as the stock reduces. Remember that stock is the foundation for other foods, such as sauces and soups, and that knowing what's in a stock is just as important as knowing how it will be used later on.

BASIC VEGETABLE STOCK

Sachet

1 bay leaf

1 teaspoon dried oregano leaves

4 sprigs parsley

1 piece of cheesecloth, cut into a 6-inch square

1 piece of butcher's twine, cut 12 inches long

2 leeks, cleaned

1 medium yellow onion, peeled

2 stalks celery

2 small carrots, peeled

1 turnip, peeled

1 parsnip, peeled

1 medium unpeeled potato

½ pound mushrooms

2 tablespoons vegetable oil

9 cloves garlic, crushed

2 tablespoons miso (fermented soy bean paste)

½ teaspoon ground white pepper

10 cups cold water

Step 1.   To make sachet, place the bay leaf, oregano and parsley in the square of cheesecloth. Gather up the corners and twist together. Using just one end of the string, tie the sachet closed. The other end of the string (the long end) will be suspended from the handle of the stockpot.

Step 2.   Cut the leeks, onion and celery into ½-inch pieces. Then slice the carrots, turnip and parsnip into ½-inch rounds. Cut the potatoes into quarters and then cut the mushrooms in half.

Step 3.   Heat the oil in a heavy, 6-quart stockpot. When the oil is hot, add the leeks, onions and carrots. Cook over medium heat, stirring occasionally, for about 5 minutes.

Step 4.   Add the celery, parsnip, turnip, potato and mushrooms. Then add the garlic, miso, ground white pepper and cold water, stirring to combine.

Step 5.   Drop in the pre-made sachet, tying the string to one handle of the stockpot. Bring to a boil, skimming off any impurities from the surface.

Step 6.   Reduce the heat and simmer, uncovered, for 30 to 35 minutes. Continue to skim off any impurities, as needed.

Step 7.   Untie the sachet. Then pour stock (and sachet) into a strainer or china cap lined with several layers of dampened cheesecloth. Use a ladle or large spoon to gently press any remaining vegetables through the strainer. Discard the sachet.

Step 8.   Allow the strained stock to cool completely. Then cover and store in the refrigerator in an air-tight container for up to 1 week. Stock may also be frozen for up to 3 months.

Yield: About 8 cups

BASIC CHICKEN STOCK

Sachet

2   bay leaves

10 parsley stems (no leaves)

½   teaspoon dried thyme leaves

12 to 14 whole black peppercorns

1   piece of cheesecloth, cut into a 6-inch square

1   piece of butcher's twine, cut 12 inches long

3   pounds chicken bones (wings, back and necks)

2   large onions, peeled

2   large carrots, peeled

2   stalks celery

4   quarts cold water

Step 1.   To make sachet, place the bay leaves, parsley stems, thyme, and black peppercorns in the square of cheesecloth. Gather up the corners and twist together. Using just one end of the string, tie the sachet closed. The other end of string (the long end) will be suspended from the handle of the stockpot.

Step 2.   Rinse bones well under cold running water.

Step 3.   Cut the onions, carrots and celery into large (¾-inch) dice.

Step 4.   Place the bones in a heavy, 6-quart stockpot. Add the onions, carrots and celery and pour in the cold water. There should be enough to completely cover the bones.

Step 5.   Drop in the pre-made sachet, tying the string to one handle of the stockpot. Bring to a boil, skimming off any impurities from the surface.

Step 6.   Reduce heat and simmer, uncovered for 2 to 3 hours, skimming off any impurities from the surface, as needed.

Step 7.   Untie the sachet. Then pour stock (and sachet) into a strainer or china cap lined with several layers of dampened cheesecloth. Use a ladle or large spoon to gently press any remaining vegetables through the strainer. Discard the bones and sachet.

Step 8.   Allow the strained stock to cool completely. Then cover and store in the refrigerator in an airtight container for up to 1 week. Stock may also be frozen for up to 3 months.

Yield: About 10 cups

BASIC FISH STOCK

Sachet

2   bay leaves

8   parsley stems (no leaves)

½   teaspoon dried thyme leaves

14   to 18 whole black peppercorns

1   piece of cheesecloth, cut into a 6-inch square

1   piece of butcher's twine, cut 12 inches long

2   pounds fish bones, tails and heads (gills removed)

1   tablespoon butter

1   small onion, peeled

1   stalk celery

½   cup dry white wine

7   to 8 cups cold water

Step 1.   To make sachet, place the bay leaves, parsley stems, thyme and black peppercorns in the square of cheesecloth. Gather up the corners and twist together. Using just one end of the string, tie the sachet closed. The other end of the string (the long end) will be suspended from the handle of the stockpot.

Step 2.   Clean the fish bones *thoroughly* under running water. Cut the onion and the celery into small (¼-inch) dice.

Step 3.   Melt the butter in a heavy, 6-quart stockpot. When hot, add the onion and celery. Sweat the vegetables over medium heat, stirring occasionally, for 3 to 5 minutes or until onion is translucent.

Step 4.   Place the bones on top of the vegetables and cover with a piece of parchment paper. Reduce heat to low and sweat the bones for about 5 minutes or until they turn opaque. Remove and discard parchment paper.

Step 5.   Add the wine and bring to a simmer. Then add the water–it should be enough to cover the bones completely.

Step 6.   Drop in the pre-made sachet, tying the string to one handle of the stockpot. Simmer, uncovered, for 25 to 30 minutes, skimming off any impurities from the surface.

Step 7.   Untie the sachet. Then pour stock (and sachet) into a strainer or china cap lined with several layers of dampened cheesecloth. Use a ladle or large spoon to gently press any remaining vegetables through the strainer. Discard the bones and sachet.

Step 8.   Allow the strained stock to cool completely. Then cover and store in the refrigerator in an airtight container for up to 1 week. Stock may also be frozen for up to 3 months.

Yield: About 6 cups

BASIC BEEF STOCK

Sachet

2 bay leaves

10 parsley stems (no leaves)

4 cloves garlic

½ teaspoon whole black peppercorns

½ teaspoon dried thyme leaves

1 piece cheesecloth, cut into a
   6-inch square

1 piece butcher's twine, cut 12 inches long

4 pounds beef bones (including marrow),
   cut into 3 to 4-inch pieces

2 unpeeled onions

2 unpeeled carrots

2 stalks celery

2 tablespoons tomato paste

4 quarts cold water

Step 1. Preheat oven to 350°F. To make sachet, place the bay leaves, parsley stems, garlic, black peppercorns and thyme in the square of cheesecloth. Gather up the corners and twist together. Using just one end of the string, tie the sachet closed. The other end of the string (the long end) will be suspended from the handle of the stockpot.

Step 2. Place the bones in roasting pan in the oven for about 30 minutes.

Step 3. Meanwhile, cut the onions, carrots and celery into 2-inch pieces. When bones have roasted for 30 minutes, remove pan from oven and add onions, carrots and celery. Return to oven and roast for about 20 minutes longer.

Step 4. Brush the bones with tomato paste, coating all sides, and return pan to oven for 15 to 20 minutes longer.

Step 5. Transfer bones and vegetables to a heavy, 8-quart stockpot. Drain off the fat from roasting pan. Using a little water to loosen the brown particles on the bottom of the roasting pan, deglaze the pan and transfer that liquid to the stockpot.

Step 6. Cover bones and vegetables with remaining cold water. Drop in the pre-made sachet, tying the string to one handle of the stockpot. Bring to a boil, skimming off any impurities from the surface.

Step 7. Reduce heat and simmer, uncovered, for 4 to 6 hours, skimming off any impurities from the surface, as needed.

Step 8. Untie the sachet. Then pour stock (and sachet) into a strainer or china cap lined with several layers of dampened cheesecloth. Use a ladle or large spoon to gently press any remaining vegetables through the strainer. Discard the bones and sachet.

Step 9. Allow the strained stock to cool completely. Then cover and store in the refrigerator in an airtight container for up to 1 week. Stock may also be frozen for up to 3 months.

Yield: About 4 cups

A WORD ABOUT SAUCES

A perfect sauce is described as the "glorious refinement of any great meal." That's pretty impressive when you consider that sauces had a rather dubious beginning. Culinary historians tell us that their primary use, before refrigeration existed, was to disguise the taste of food rather than enhance it.

We give credit to the French for developing the intricate classification system of sauces used today. Grouped in "families" according to ingredients and method of preparation, their classification is broken down further—the savory from the sweet sauces, the hot from the cold, and so on.

Once you understand the "lineage" of a sauce within its family, in other words, once you understand how it is prepared, you can change and refine the taste of any sauce with great success.

For example, the classic *suprême sauce* is an offspring of one of the five "primary sauces", in this case a *velouté* (page 36). This particular *velouté* is made with chicken stock, but if you substituted fish stock and added a reduction of minced shallots and white wine, you would have made *bercy sauce* instead.

In addition to the classic sauces developed by the French, many innovative restaurants today prepare an array of exciting sauces—full-flavored wine reductions, delicate vinaigrettes and infused oils made with fresh seasonal herbs and sweet dessert sauces made with exotic ingredients in unusual combinations.

Cooks at home cook can do the same, even without a recipe, by following three ingredients for successful sauce-making: (1) familiarize yourself with the "family of sauces", in particular how a sauce is made, (2) choose the freshest ingredients you can possibly find, and (3) remember that the best sauces, whether simple or complex, have well-balanced flavor and enough character to stand on their own.

BASIC BECHAMEL SAUCE

4   cups whole milk or cream
4   tablespoons clarified butter
4   tablespoons all-purpose flour
1   small onion, peeled
3   whole cloves

3   whole bay leaves
¼   teaspoon salt
⅛   teaspoon ground white pepper
⅛   teaspoon freshly ground nutmeg

Step 1.   Place the milk in a heavy saucepan and heat until scalded.

Step 2.   Heat the clarified butter in a heavy 2-quart saucepan over medium heat. Whisk in the flour (to a paste consistency) and cook, stirring constantly, for 2 to 3 minutes, until the roux bubbles and begins to color slightly. This is called a *light roux*.

Step 3.   Very gradually, stir in the scalded milk, whisking continuously until smooth.

Step 4.   Bring to a boil over medium heat. Then reduce heat and begin to simmer sauce.

Step 5.   Meanwhile, slice the onion in half lengthwise. Using only half the onion, pierce a whole clove through a bay leaf and then attach it to one side of the onion. Repeat with the two remaining cloves and bay leaves, attaching them around the edges of the onion. The onion will be used to flavor the sauce.

Step 6.   Place the studded onion in the sauce and simmer, uncovered, for 15 to 20 minutes, stirring occasionally.

Step 7.   Remove and discard studded onion. Adjust the consistency of the sauce with additional hot milk, if necessary. Season to taste with salt, white pepper and freshly ground nutmeg.

Step 8.   Strain the sauce through a fine strainer or china cap lined with cheesecloth.

Step 9.   Set over a double boiler filled with warm water until ready to serve. If not using immediately, dab the top of the sauce with some butter to prevent a skin from forming.

Yield: About 4 cups

BASIC VELOUTE SAUCE

2 cups Basic Chicken Stock (page 31) or Basic Fish Stock (page 32)

3 tablespoons butter

3 tablespoons all-purpose flour

⅛ teaspoon salt

⅛ teaspoon ground white pepper

Step 1. Place the stock in a small saucepan and bring to a boil. Turn off the heat and set aside.

Step 2. Melt the butter in a heavy, 2-quart saucepan over low heat.

Step 3. Whisk in the flour (to a paste consistency) and cook over medium heat, stirring constantly, for 2 to 3 minutes until the roux bubbles and begins to color slightly.

Step 4. Remove the roux from the heat and allow to cool slightly. Then gradually pour in the hot stock, whisking continuously until smooth.

Step 5. Return pan to heat, bring to a boil over medium heat, whisking constantly.

Step 6. Reduce heat and simmer, uncovered, for about 5 minutes.

Step 7. Season to taste with salt and white pepper, if desired.

Step 8. Set over a double boiler filled with warm water until ready to serve. If not using immediately, dab the top of the sauce with some butter to prevent a skin from forming.

Yield: About 2 cups

VARIATIONS

Suprême Sauce: Pour **1 quart Chicken Velouté** into a heavy, 2-quart saucepan and simmer over low heat until reduced by one-fourth. Place **1 cup milk** in a bowl. Slowly add ½ cup of the hot velouté to the milk, stirring constantly. Stir the mixture back into the pan and bring to a simmer. Cut **¼ pound butter** into pieces and drop them, one at a time, into the sauce while stirring constantly. Add **1 teaspoon lemon juice** and adjust seasonings, as needed. If desired, strain the sauce through a fine strainer (or cheesecloth) and serve immediately. **Yield: About 2 cups**

Hungarian Sauce: Melt **2 tablespoons butter** in heavy saucepan over medium heat. Add **1 small minced onion** and **1 tablespoon paprika**. Sweat the onion, stirring occasionally, for 3 to 4 minutes or until soft. Add **½ cup dry white wine** and continue to cook for about 3 more minutes or until mixture is reduced by one-half. Stir in **2 cups Chicken Velouté** and simmer for 10 minutes. Strain the sauce through a fine strainer (or cheesecloth) and serve immediately. **Yield: About 2 cups**

Curry Sauce: Melt **2 tablespoons butter** in a heavy saucepan over medium heat. Add **1 small minced onion, 1 stalk diced celery** and **1 small diced carrot**. Sweat the vegetables over medium heat, stirring occasionally, for about 3 to 5 minutes until tender. Stir in **1 tablespoon curry powder, 1 clove minced garlic, a pinch of dried thyme, ½ bay leaf** and **4 parsley stems**. Cook for about 1 minute. Add **1 quart Chicken** or **Fish Velouté**. Reduce heat and simmer for 20 minutes. Stir in **½ cup milk** or **cream** until blended. If desired, strain the sauce through a fine strainer (or cheesecloth) and then add **1 teaspoon lemon juice**. Serve immediately. **Yield: About 3 cups**

Bercy Sauce: Place **1 cup dry white wine** and **2 minced shallots** in a heavy, 2-quart saucepan and cook over moderate heat for 5 to 7 minutes or until reduced by three-fourths. Add **1 quart Fish Velouté**, reduce heat and simmer for 10 minutes. Stir in **1 tablespoon unsalted butter** and **3 tablespoons finely chopped parsley**. Serve immediately. **Yield: About 4 cups**

BASIC BROWN SAUCE/SAUCE ESPAGÑOLE

Sachet
½ bay leaf
2 parsley stems (no leaves)
⅛ teaspoon dried thyme leaves
1 clove garlic
1 piece cheesecloth, cut into a 6-inch square
1 piece butcher's twine, cut 12 inches long

1 small onion, peeled
1 carrot, peeled

1 stalk celery
½ cup clarified butter
½ cup all-purpose flour
2 tablespoons additional clarified butter
6 cups Basic Beef Stock (page 33), brought to room temperature
2 ounces tomato purée
⅛ teaspoon salt
⅛ teaspoon ground white pepper

Step 1. To make sachet, place the bay leaf, parsley stems, thyme and garlic in the square of cheese-cloth. Gather up the corners and twist together. Using just one end of the string, tie the sachet closed. The other end of the string (the long end) will be suspended from the handle of the saucepan.

Step 2. Cut the onion, carrot and celery into medium (½-inch) dice. Set aside.

Step 3. Heat the ½ cup of clarified butter in small saucepan until hot. Whisk in the flour (to a paste consistency) and cook over medium heat, stirring constantly, for 8 to 10 minutes until the roux bubbles, turns light-brown in color and has a nutty aroma. This is called a *dark roux*. Set aside.

Step 4. Place the remaining 2 tablespoons clarified butter in heavy, 4-quart stockpot over medium heat.

Step 5. Add the onion, carrot and celery. Sauté the vegetables, stirring often, for about 6 to 8 minutes or until well browned.

Step 6. Add the cooked roux to the vegetables, stirring to combine.

Step 7. Gradually, pour in the brown stock and then the tomato purée.

Step 8. Tie the pre-made sachet to one handle of the stockpot, letting it dangle in the liquid.

Step 9. Bring to a boil, skimming off any impurities from the surface, as needed.

Step 10. Reduce heat and simmer, uncovered, for about 2 hours, skimming the surface occasionally, until the sauce is reduced to about 1 quart.

Step 11. Untie sachet. Then pour sauce (and sachet) into a fine strainer or china cap lined with cheesecloth. Use a ladle or spoon to gently press any remaining vegetables through the strainer. Discard the sachet.

Step 12. Season to taste with salt and white pepper, if desired.

Step 13. Set over a double boiler filled with warm water until ready to serve. Or, cool completely, then cover and store in the refrigerator in an airtight container for up to 1 week. Sauce may also be frozen for up to 3 months.

Yield: About 1 quart

VARIATIONS

Demi-glace: A "brown stock" is simply a stock made with roasted bones, rather than bones that have only been rinsed and/or blanched prior to use. To make a brown stock, you can use roasted beef or veal bones or roasted chicken bones. In this recipe, we are calling for a brown stock made with roasted beef bones (see Basic Beef Stock, page 33). Place **4 cups Brown Stock** and **4 cups Brown Sauce/Sauce Espagñole** in a heavy, 3-quart saucepan. Bring to a boil over medium heat, stirring occasionally. Reduce heat and simmer, uncovered, for 15 to 20 minutes or until the sauce is reduced by one half. Remove from heat. Pour sauce through a fine strainer or china cap lined with cheesecloth. Allow to cool completely. Then cover and store in the refrigerator in an airtight container for up to 1 week. Sauce may also be frozen for up to 3 months. **Yield: 1 quart**

Bordelaise Sauce: Place **1 cup red wine, 2 minced shallots, ¼ teaspoon crushed black peppercorns, pinch of thyme** and **½ bay leaf** in a saucepan. Bring to a boil and then reduce to medium heat. Cook for about 33 minutes or until reduced by three-fourths. Add **1 quart Demi-glace** (see above) and simmer for 15 to 20 minutes. Remove from the heat and strain through a fine strainer (or cheesecloth). Cut 2 **tablespoons butter** into small pieces and drop them, one at a time, into the sauce while stirring constantly to combine. Serve immediately. **Yield: About 4 cups**

Madeira Sauce: Place **1 quart Demi-glace** (see above) in a heavy saucepan over medium heat. Cook for 30 to 45 minutes or until reduced to ½ cup. Add **¼ cup Madeira wine**, stirring to combine. Serve immediately. **Yield: About 4 cups**

Mushroom Sauce: Melt **1 tablespoon butter** in heavy sauté pan over moderate heat. Add **1 minced shallot** and sauté for 2 to 3 minutes until translucent. Add **½ pound sliced mushrooms** and continue sautéing until brown. Add **1 quart Demi-glace** (see above) and simmer for about 10 minutes. Add **1 tablespoon dry sherry** and **1 teaspoon lemon juice**. Serve immediately. **Yield: About 4 cups**

BASIC TOMATO SAUCE

Sachet
1   bay leaf
1   clove garlic, crushed
1   sprig thyme
1   whole clove
5   black peppercorns, crushed
1   piece cheesecloth, cut into a 6-inch square
1   piece butcher's twine, cut 12 inches long

1   tablespoon clarified butter
2   ounces salt pork, diced

½   small onion, peeled
1   carrot, peeled
1   stalk celery
2   ounces all-purpose flour
3   cups Basic Chicken Stock (page 31) or Basic Vegetable Stock (page 30)
2   cups tomato purée (or substitute 2 to 3 cups chopped tomatoes for one cup of the purée)
⅛   teaspoon salt
⅛   teaspoon ground white pepper

Step 1.   To make sachet, place the bay leaf, garlic, thyme, clove, and black peppercorns in the square of the cheesecloth. Gather up the corners and twist together. Using one end of the string, tie the sachet closed. The other end of the string (the long end) will be suspended from the handle of the saucepan.

Step 2.   Heat the clarified butter in a heavy 4-quart saucepan over moderate heat. Add the salt pork and sauté for 3 to 4 minutes or until pork is partially rendered.

Step 3.   Add the onion, carrot and celery. Reduce heat to medium and cook, stirring occasionally, for 3 to 5 minutes or until the onions are translucent.

Step 4.   Add the flour, stirring to combine. Cook, stirring often, for 3 to 5 minutes or until the roux is light brown in color.

Step 5.   Slowly add the stock until combined. Then add the tomato purée.

Step 6.   Tie the pre-made sachet to one handle of the saucepan, letting it dangle in the liquid.

Step 7.   Bring back to a boil. Then reduce heat and simmer, uncovered, for one hour or until sauce has thickened to desired consistency.

Step 8.   Untie the sachet. Then pour stock (and sachet) through a fine strainer or china cap lined with cheesecloth. Use a ladle or spoon to gently press any remaining vegetables through the strainer. Discard sachet.

Step 9.   Season to taste with salt and white pepper, if desired.

Step 10. Keep warm until ready to serve. Or cool completely, then cover and store in the refrigerator in an airtight container for up to 1 week. Sauce may be also frozen for up to 3 months.

Yield: About 6 cups

VARIATIONS

Creole Sauce: Heat a heavy saucepan over moderate heat. When pan is hot, add **2 tablespoons safflower oil**. When oil is hot, add **1 small diced onion, 1 thinly-sliced stalk celery, 1 small diced green pepper** and **1 clove chopped garlic.** Sauté lightly for 3 to 5 minutes or until onion is translucent. Add **1 quart Basic Tomato Sauce, 1 bay leaf, a pinch of thyme** and **½ teaspoon lemon zest.** Reduce heat and simmer, uncovered, for 10 minutes. Serve immediately or keep warm until ready to serve. **Yield: About 4 cups**

Portuguese Sauce: Heat a heavy saucepan over moderate heat. When pan is hot, add **2 tablespoons safflower oil.** When oil is hot, add **1 small diced onion** and sauté for 2 to 3 minutes or until translucent. Add **3 medium, finely-diced tomatoes** and **1 clove minced garlic.** Simmer, uncovered, for 10 to 12 minutes or until reduced by one-third. Stir in **1 quart Basic Tomato Sauce** and **3 tablespoons chopped parsley.** Simmer for 10 minutes longer. Serve immediately or keep warm until ready to serve. **Yield: About 4 cups**

Spanish Sauce: Heat a heavy saucepan over moderate heat. When pan is hot, add **2 tablespoons safflower oil.** When oil is hot, add **1 small diced onion, 2 small diced green peppers** and **1 clove minced garlic.** Lightly sauté but take care *not to brown.* Add **¼ pound sliced mushrooms** and sauté for 1 to 2 minutes longer or until soft. Add **1 quart Basic Tomato Sauce** and simmer, uncovered, for 10 minutes longer. Season to taste with **salt, white pepper,** and **hot red pepper sauce.** Serve immediately or keep warm until ready to serve. **Yield: About 4 cups**

HOLLANDAISE

3 egg yolks	⅛ teaspoon cayenne pepper
3 tablespoons water	⅛ teaspoon salt
¼ teaspoon fresh lemon juice, strained	¾ cup clarified butter (keep warm)

Step 1. In the top of a double boiler, whisk together egg yolks, water, lemon juice, cayenne and salt.

Step 2. Cook over low heat, whisking vigorously, until mixture is creamy and reaches the ribbon stage.

Step 3. Remove mixture from heat but continue whisking. Add the clarified butter, *very slowly at first*, by dropping in no more than 1 teaspoonful at a time.

Step 4. After a total of 2 to 3 tablespoons of butter have been whisked in and absorbed, add the remaining butter in a slow, very thin stream. Continue whisking vigorously.

Step 5. Taste and adjust seasoning as desired.

Step 6. Sauce may be kept warm for 15 minutes over a double boiler on very low heat. The water should not exceed 150°F. If the sauce separates, place one egg yolk in a clean pan over a double boiler filled with 150°F water. Whisk to a light froth. Remove from heat and slowly add the separated sauce to the cooked egg yolk, whisking vigorously until completely combined.

Yield: 1 cup

VARIATION

Bernaise Sauce: Place ¼ **cup white wine vinegar, 1 tablespoon minced shallots, ½ teaspoon dried tarragon** and ¼ **teaspoon freshly ground black pepper** in a heavy, 1-quart saucepan over moderate heat. Gently boil for 3 to 4 minutes or until mixture is reduced to about 2 tablespoons. Add 1 cup **Hollandaise Sauce,** stirring to combine. Strain into a double boiler and reheat. **Yield: About 1 cup**

BASIC MAYONNAISE

1   whole egg
2   egg yolks
1½ teaspoon Dijon-style mustard
¼   teaspoon salt

1   tablespoon lemon juice, tarragon or
    wine vinegar
    Freshly ground white pepper
1½ to 2 cups peanut oil or good-quality
    olive oil

Step 1.   Place the egg yolks and mustard in the bowl of a food processor fitted with a metal blade. Process with on/off bursts for about 30 seconds or until blended.

Step 2.   Add the salt and lemon juice and process for about 15 seconds longer.

Step 3.   This next step is *very critical and it must be done slowly.* With the machine running, add just a few drops of oil to begin with. Continue adding oil, a few drops at a time, in a slow steady stream.

Step 4.   As the mixture begins to thicken slightly, begin to add the oil a little faster. You should still be adding the oil slowly in a steady stream. Continue adding oil until all has been incorporated and the mixture has emulsified.

Step 5.   Adjust the flavor of the mayonnaise as needed. If the mayonnaise appears too stiff, add a few drops of water, stirring to combine. Transfer to an airtight container and store in the refrigerator for up to 4 days.

Step 6.   Note: If you add the oil too fast or the mayonnaise separates, place an egg yolk in a small bowl and whisk in the separated mayonnaise, just a little at a time. Continue to whisk vigorously, adding small amounts of mayonnaise each time, until mixture has thickened.

Yield: About 2 cups

VARIATIONS

Herbed Mayonnaise: Prepare Basic Mayonnaise as directed. Transfer 2 to 3 tablespoons into a small bowl and stir in **2 teaspoons minced garlic** and ¼ cup (*total*) of any 3 of the following: **minced chervil, parsley, tarragon, dill, basil or Italian parsley**. Return the herbed mayonnaise into bowl of mayonnaise, stirring to combine. Cover and store in the refrigerator an airtight container for up to 4 days. **Yield: About 2 cups**

Andalouse Mayonnaise: Prepare Basic Mayonnaise as directed. Add ⅓ **cup tomato purée** or minced pimentoes and ½ **teaspoon ground cayenne pepper**. Cover and store in the refrigerator an airtight container for up to 4 days. **Yield: About 2 cups**

RELISHES & SALSAS

Tomatillo Relish

2 medium tomatoes

7 to 8 tomatillos

4 cloves garlic, peeled

¼ cup red wine vinegar

1 teaspoon fennel seed

½ cup olive oil

Salt

Freshly ground white pepper

Step 1. To blanch tomatoes, score an "X" on the bottom of each tomato and place in a large pan of boiling water to blanch for 15 seconds. Remove tomatoes with a slotted spoon and plunge them into a bowl of ice water. Then peel the tomatoes and cut into small (¼-inch) dice. Place in a small bowl.

Step 2. Remove thin skin (paper) from the tomatillos and cut into very small (⅛-inch) dice. Minced the garlic. Add garlic and tomatillos to the tomato concassée, stirring to combine.

Step 3. Stir in the vinegar, fennel seeds and olive oil. Season to taste with salt and white pepper.

Yield: About 3 cups

VARIATIONS

Tomato-Corn Relish: Combine **2 cups tomato concassée, 1 cup roasted corn kernels, ½ cup red wine vinegar, 1 bunch chopped cilantro** and **1 cup peanut oil** in a small bowl. Cover and refrigerate for up to 4 days. **Yield: About 3½ cups**

Three Pepper Relish: Combine, seed and finely dice **2 medium red peppers, 2 medium yellow peppers,** and **2 medium green peppers**. Add **½ cup red wine vinegar, ¼ bunch chopped basil leaves, ¼ bunch chopped Italian parsley leaves, ½ cup olive oil**, and **salt** and **ground white pepper**. Cover and refrigerate for up to 4 days. **Yield: About 3 cups**

Citrus Salsa: Cut the peel off a **1 pink grapefruit**. Using a sharp knife, cut out each section and remove seeds, taking care to remove all the pith and membrane. Repeat procedure with **3 tangerines**. Drain grapefruit and tangerines in a colander for about 5 minutes. Coarsely chop the grapefruit and tangerine section and place in a bowl. Add **¼ cup finely diced jicama, 2 to 3 tablespoons fresh lime juice, ¼ bunch fresh mint leaves** (cut into a *chiffonade*), **1 to 2 teaspoons honey, ¼ teaspoon dried red chile peppers** and **salt** to taste. Cover and refrigerate for up to 4 days. **Yield: About 2½ cups**

STARTERS

CHESTNUT & CARROT SOUP
WITH CREME FRAICHE & CHERVIL

Crème fraîche
¼ cup sour cream
2 cups heavy cream

2 to 3 pounds carrots, peeled
1 onion, peeled
12 ounces canned chestnuts, drained
3 tablespoons canola oil

1½ quarts Basic Chicken Stock (page 31)
1 potato, peeled
2 tablespoons brown sugar
Pinch of cayenne pepper
1 cup half-and-half

Sprigs of fresh chervil

Step 1. To make crème fraîche, combine the sour cream and heavy cream in a small bowl. Allow to stand at room temperature (75° to 90°F) for about 24 hours.

Step 2. If you want a thicker crème fraîche, whip the mixture briefly to desired consistency. Or, cover and refrigerate for up to 3 days.

Step 3. To make soup, coarsely chop the onion, carrots, potato and chestnuts.

Step 4. Heat oil in a heavy 3-quart saucepan over moderate heat. Add onions and carrots and sweat for 1 to 2 minutes or until onions are transparent.

Step 5. Add the potato and chestnuts and sauté for 2 minutes.

Step 6. Add stock, brown sugar and cayenne. Reduce heat and simmer, uncovered for 25 to 30 minutes or until potatoes are tender and soup has been reduced by one-half.

Step 7. Whirl mixture in a food processor fitted with a metal blade until smooth. Return to saucepan and reheat.

Step 8. Lightly whisk the half-and-half into the soup to lighten the texture and extend the volume.

Step 9. Adjust seasonings and serve in individual bowls. Garnish with fresh chervil and crème fraîche, if desired.

Yield: About 4 servings (Pictured on page 87.)

GRILLED VEGETABLE GAZPACHO
WITH BLACK PEPPERCORN & ONION GARNISH

1   large onion, peeled
2   zucchini
1   each red, yellow and green pepper
      (or any combination)
⅔   cup olive oil
8   vine-ripened tomatoes
3   cucumbers
8   cloves garlic, peeled
½   cup fresh sourdough breadcrumbs
½   cup red wine vinegar

2   cups tomato juice
   Salt and pepper

Garnish
2   tablespoons thinly-sliced scallions
      (tops only), cut on the bias
2   tablespoons finely diced red onion
      Coarsely ground black pepper

Step 1.   Preheat the grill, according to manufacturer's directions. The temperature of the grill should be moderately hot.

Step 2.   Cut onion into thirds lengthwise. Trim off ends of zucchini and slice in half lengthwise. Brush onion, zucchini and whole peppers with a little olive oil and arrange on the grill over high heat.

Step 3.   Grill, turning occasionally, for 3 to 4 minutes per side or until the skin of the peppers blister and turn black and the vegetables are roasted. Remove and set aside to cool.

Step 4.   Peel the blistered skin off with a knife. Cut peppers in half and remove the seeds and membrane. Cut all vegetables and place in the bowl of a food processor fitted with a metal blade. Process until coarsely chopped and transfer to a bowl.

Step 5.   Core tomatoes and cut into medium (½-inch) dice. Peel the cucumbers and cut into medium (½-inch) dice. Finely chop the garlic.

Step 6.   Add tomatoes, cucumbers, garlic and breadcrumbs with the vegetables. Stir in the vinegar and tomato juice.

Step 7.   Gradually, add the remaining olive oil, stirring to combine.

Step 8.   Refrigerate for 2 to 3 hours until well chilled. Garnish the edges of the plate with the scallions, red onion and coarsely ground black pepper.

Yield: About 6 servings (Pictured on page 85.)

FOUR ONION SOUP
WITH FRIED GREEN ONION STRINGS

Garnish
2 bunches green onions, cleaned and dry
   Vegetable oil, for frying

Soup
2 bunches scallions, cleaned
6 shallots, peeled
3 cloves garlic
1 red onion, peeled

2 yellow onions, peeled
3 tablespoons olive oil
1 quart Basic Chicken Stock (page 31)
¾ cup dry white wine
1 tablespoon fresh thyme leaves
1 teaspoon ground white pepper
2 cups half-and-half
⅛ teaspoon salt

Step 1.   Cut off and reserve top green portion of the scallions; then coarsely chop the white portion. Chop the shallots and crush the garlic. Thinly slice the red and yellow onions.

Step 2.   Heat the olive oil in a heavy, 2-quart saucepan over moderate heat. When oil is hot, add the shallots and white portion of the scallions and sauté for 3 to 4 minutes or until tender.

Step 3.   Add the garlic and sliced red and yellow onions and sauté for 3 to 4 minutes longer or until garlic is light brown in color.

Step 4.   Add the chicken stock, wine, thyme and white pepper, stirring to combine. Reduce heat and simmer, uncovered, for 30 to 40 minutes or until soup is reduced by one-half. Stir in the half-and-half, reduce heat to low and simmer, uncovered, for an additional 30 minutes.

Step 5.   To make garnish, meanwhile, cut the reserved scallion tops lengthwise into very thin strings, about 6 inches long. You should have about 1 cup.

Step 6.   Heat about 1 cup oil in a heavy sauté pan over moderate heat. When oil is very hot, drop a small handful of onion strings into the pan and fry, turning occasionally with tongs or wire strainer, for 2 to 3 minutes or until lightly crispy. Remove and drain on paper towels.

Step 7.   Remove soup from the heat and blend to a silky texture using a hand blender or food processor.

Step 8.   Adjust the seasonings with salt and pepper to taste. Ladle soup into individual bowls and garnish each with a mound of fried onion strings.

Yield: 4 to 6 servings

COUNTRY-STYLE PISTACHIO PATE WITH
MARINATED VEGETABLES & CORNICHONS

MARINATED CALAMARI & PRAWN
SALAD WITH CAVIAR VINAIGRETTE

LAYERED CARROT, CAULIFLOWER &
BROCCOLI TERRINE WITH SAUCE VERTE

BOUQUET SALAD OF FARM GREENS
WITH HERBED GOAT CHEESE TIMBALES

PUMPKIN SOUP
WITH HERBED CROUTONS

Herbed Croutons

½   loaf (1 lb.) French bread

3   to 4 tablespoons fresh herbs (choose from: thyme leaves, Italian parsley, oregano leaves and marjoram leaves)

3   tablespoons melted butter

1   small onion, peeled

1   medium potato, peeled

1   large clove garlic, peeled

2   tablespoons butter

4   cups Basic Chicken Stock (page 31)

4   cups coarsely-chopped fresh pumpkin or Hubbard squash (skin removed)

1   cup half-and-half or milk

1   teaspoon ground nutmeg

½   teaspoon ground mace

Step 1   To make croutons, preheat oven to 275°F. Cut bread into medium (½-inch) cubes. Scatter bread evenly on a rimmed baking sheet and bake for 10 minutes.

Step 2.   Meanwhile, place fresh herbs in a mincer/chopper and process until finely chopped. Add to the melted butter, stirring to combine. Remove croutons from oven and toss in a bowl with the herbed butter. Place buttered croutons back on baking sheet and toast in oven for 25 to 30 minutes longer or until lightly browned. Remove and set aside.

Step 3.   To prepare soup, chop onion and potato into small (¼-inch) dice. Mince the garlic. Melt the butter in a heavy, 3-quart saucepan over medium heat. When butter is melted, add onions, potatoes and garlic and sweat vegetables for 4 to 5 minutes.

Step 4.   Add 3 cups of the chicken stock, bring to a boil and cook, uncovered, for 4 to 5 minutes or until slightly reduced. Add the pumpkin and simmer for 25 to 30 minutes or until tender.

Step 5.   Remove from heat. Using a hand blender, process pumpkin mixture until puréed. Return pan to low heat, stir in remaining stock, half-and-half, nutmeg and mace. Simmer, uncovered, for 5 to 10 minutes or until heated through.

Step 6.   Pour into a soup tureen and offer bowl of herbed croutons as an accompaniment.

Yield: 6 to 8 servings

ROASTED EGGPLANT SOUP

4	medium eggplants	3	cups Basic Chicken Stock (page 31)
3	to 4 tablespoons olive oil	1	tablespoon chopped fresh rosemary
4	large tomatoes		Salt and ground black pepper
2	cloves garlic, peeled		

Step 1.   Preheat the oven to 400°F. Slice the eggplant in half lengthwise and place on a baking sheet. Score the flesh of each half with a sharp knife in 5 or 6 places.

Step 2.   Brush the flesh with about 1 tablespoon of the olive oil and bake in the oven for about 40 minutes or until tender and golden brown. Set aside to cool.

Step 3.   To blanch tomatoes, score an "X" on the bottom of each tomato and place in a large pan of boiling water to blanch for 15 seconds. Remove tomatoes with a slotted spoon and plunge them into a bowl of ice water. Then peel the tomatoes. Squeeze out seeds and coarsely chop. Mince the garlic.

Step 4.   Scoop out the eggplant flesh and set aside. Heat remaining oil in a heavy, 3-quart saucepan over moderate heat. When oil is hot, add the garlic and tomatoes and sauté for 5 to 6 minutes. Add the eggplant, stirring to combine.

Step 5.   Add the chicken stock. Reduce heat and cook, stirring occasionally, for 20 minutes.

Step 6.   Using the hand blender, process the soup until a smooth consistency is reached. Season with chopped rosemary and salt and pepper to taste.

Yield: About 6 servings

FIVE PEA SOUP WITH
PEPPERED BEEF JERKY

4　ounces black-eye beans (soaked 24 hrs.)
4　ounces chick peas (soaked 24 hrs.)
4　ounces green split peas
4　ounces golden split peas
8　ounces green peas (English)
6　ribs celery
2　onions, peeled
2　carrots, peeled
2　tablespoons vegetable oil
7　cups Basic Chicken Stock (page 31)
4　cloves garlic, crushed

2　bay leaves
2　teaspoons ground black pepper

Jerky
¾　pound top round steak
2　teaspoons salt
2　tablespoons brown sugar
2　tablespoons onion powder
1　teaspoon garlic powder
2　teaspoons coarsely cracked black pepper
¼　cup vegetable oil

Step 1.　To make soup, presoak black-eye beans and chick peas in enough water to cover for 24 hours. Drain and rinse well. Rinse split peas and golden peas and drain well.

Step 2.　Cut the celery, onions and carrots into medium (½-inch) dice.

Step 3.　Heat oil in a heavy, 2-quart saucepan over medium heat. When oil is hot, add the celery, onions and carrots and sweat, stirring occasionally, for 2 to 3 minutes.

Step 4.　Add the five kinds of peas, stock, garlic, bay leaves, and pepper. Reduce heat and simmer, uncovered, for 2 to 3 hours until peas are tender.

Step 5.　To make jerky, combine salt, brown sugar, onion powder, garlic powder, pepper and oil in a bowl forming a paste. Preheat the oven at 275°F.

Step 6.　Cut the beef across the grain into very thin slices.

Step 7.　Spread the paste mixture on both sides of each slice, cover with plastic wrap and refrigerate for about 2 hours.

Step 8.　Position a wire cooling rack inside a large cookie sheet. Arrange the marinated beef strips on the cooling rack and place in the preheated oven. (The cookie sheet will catch the drippings as the jerky bakes.) Bake the strips in a low oven for 1½ to 2 hours or until the jerky turns brown and become crisp and brittle.

Step 9.　To serve, remove bay leaves and strain soup. Adjust seasoning with salt and pepper to taste. Ladle soup into individual bowls and offer small pieces of jerky as a garnish.

Yield: About 6 servings

GRILLED CORN CHOWDER
WITH POTATO PUREE & BEET CHIPS

6 ears of corn in husks
1 large onion, peeled
2 ribs celery
1 russet potato, peeled
6 strips smoked bacon
2 cups Basic Chicken Stock (page 31)
1 teaspoon granulated sugar
1 bay leaf
3 cups half-and-half
1 cup mashed potato

Beet Chips
1 beet, trimmed and peeled
1 cup vegetable oil

Purée
¾ pound russet potato, peeled
1½ tablespoons unsalted butter
⅛ cup half-and-half

Garnish
1 tablespoon chopped chives

Step 1.   Preheat grill (or oven broiler) according to manufacturer's directions. The grill should be moderately hot.

Step 2.   To make corn, place corn on hot grill (or under broiler) over moderate heat. Grill, turning occasionally, for 20 to 25 minutes or until outside is lightly charred.

Step 3.   Remove and cool slightly. Peel off and discard husk and silk. Separate kernels from the cob, using a knife, and set aside.

Step 4.   Meanwhile, to make purée, cut potatoes into eighths and cook in boiling water for 15 to 20 minutes or until tender.

Step 5.   Drain, cool and place in a food processor along with butter and half-and-half. Process until smooth.

Step 6.   Meanwhile, to make soup, cut the onion, celery and potato into small (¼-inch) dice.

Step 7.   Cut the bacon into small (¼-inch) dice.

Step 8.   Place bacon in a heavy, 2-quart saucepan and fry until lightly browned.

Step 9.   Add the onion, celery and potato and sauté for about 2 minutes.

Step 10.   Add the corn and continue to sauté for 2 minutes longer.

Step 11. Stir in the stock, sugar and bay leaf.

Step 12. Bring to a boil, reduce heat and simmer, uncovered, for about 15 minutes.

Step 13. Meanwhile, to make beet chips, cut beet in half and then cut each half into thin slices. Lightly dust each slice with a little cornstarch; then pat off any excess.

Step 14. Heat oil in heavy saucepan over moderate heat to 350°F.

Step 15. Place beet chips in hot oil and fry for 1 to 2 minutes per side, turning once, until crisp. Drain on paper towels.

Step 16. To assemble, remove bay leaf from soup, add half-and-half and reheat to simmering.

Step 17. Ladle soup into bowls. Carefully, place a large dollop of potato purée in the center of the soup and garnish with a few fried beet chips. Sprinkle with chives, if desired.

Yield: About 6 servings

OXTAIL CONSOMME
WITH CUSTARD ROYALE

Consommé

3	pounds oxtails, cut into 2-inch lengths
1	carrot, peeled
1	small onion, peeled
2	tablespoons tomato paste
8	cups Basic Beef Stock (page 33) or water
1	leek, cleaned
1	clove garlic, crushed
¼	teaspoon dried thyme leaves
3	sprigs parsley
2	bay leaves
¼	teaspoon ground black pepper
⅛	teaspoon salt

Raft (Filter)

1	carrot, peeled and coarsely chopped
1	small onion, peeled and coarsely chopped
	Reserved oxtail meat
6	egg whites, lightly whisked

Custard

2	whole eggs
1	cup heavy cream
¼	teaspoon fresh thyme leaves
½	teaspoon fresh chives

Sherry or Madeira wine

Step 1.   To make consommé, preheat oven to 400°F. Place the oxtails into a shallow roasting pan and roast 30 to 35 minutes or until browned.

Step 2.   Cut onion and carrot into medium (½-inch) dice. Add to the roasting pan. Brush oxtails with tomato paste, return to oven and roast for 15 minutes longer.

Step 3.   Using a slotted spoon, transfer oxtails and vegetables to a 4-quart stock pot. Discard the fat and place roasting pan on a burner over moderate heat until hot.

Step 4.   Add about ¼ cup beef stock and deglaze the roasting pan by dissolving any cooked food particles remaining on the bottom. Add deglazed mixture to the stock pot. Add the leeks, garlic, thyme, parsley, bay leaf and pepper. Bring to a slow simmer and cook, uncovered, for 4 to 6 hours.

Step 5.   Pour the stock into a strainer or china cap lined with cheesecloth, reserving the oxtail meat, and discard any remaining solids. Allow to cool. Then chill in the refrigerator for 3 to 4 hours. (At this point, you may cover and store the stock in the refrigerator for up to 3 days.)

Step 6.   Remove all fat from the surface of the chilled stock. Transfer *only* the semi-clear jellied liquid into a heavy, 4-quart stockpot. Take care not to transfer any of the cloudy or muddy bottom sediment. (This sediment, however, can be reserved for other soups and sauces.)

Step 7. To make the raft, place onion and carrot in a food processor fitted with a metal blade. Process with on/off bursts for about 1 minute. Add the oxtail meat and process into a purée.

Step 8. Transfer purée to a bowl and fold in the egg whites. Set aside.

Step 9. Bring stock to a *very slow simmer over low heat*. As stock begins to heat, temper the egg white/purée by whisking in about one cup of stock until combined. Transfer back into the stockpot and whisk *ONLY* until it comes to a full simmer. *Do not stir.*

Step 10. You will notice a raft (coagulated clear protein) forming on the surface. As the raft begins to float, use a spoon to make a small hole or "vent" in the center. (The vent allows the stock to circulate. It filters the stock in an action similar to a coffee percolator.)

Step 11. Simmer until the raft is solidly formed. It should be firm enough so that when you strain the stock, the raft holds together keeping the particles intact.

Step 12. Carefully, ladle the consommé through a strainer or china cap lined with several layers of cheesecloth into a saucepan, taking care not to disturb the raft in the stockpot. Make sure to keep the end of the china cap out of the clear consommé. Keep consommé hot.

Step 13. To make custard, preheat the oven to 350°F and set a roasting pan inside.

Step 14. Whisk together the eggs, cream, thyme, chives and white pepper. Pour mixture into 8-inch baking dish; set dish inside the roasting pan.

Step 15. Carefully pour enough warm water into the roasting pan to come three-fourths of the way up the sides of the baking dish. Bake 8 to 10 minutes or until the custard sets.

Step 16. Remove custard from water bath. Allow to set for 15 to 20 minutes. Then cut custard into small dice or decorative shapes.

Step 17. To serve, pour one fourth teaspoon of sherry into each soup bowl. Ladle in some hot consommé and garnish with several pieces of custard.

Yield: 8 to 10 servings

BOUQUET SALAD
WITH HERBED CHEESE CUSTARD TIMBALES

Custard
1   tablespoon butter or margarine
3   egg yolks
3   tablespoons cornstarch
½   teaspoon granulated sugar
1   cup half-and-half
¼   cup Boursin cheese, crumbled

Vinaigrette
2   tablespoons chopped fresh cilantro
1   tablespoon minced garlic
¼   cup balsamic vinegar
2   tablespoons granulated sugar
½   cup olive oil
⅛   teaspoon salt
¼   teaspoon white pepper

Salad
4   beefsteak tomatoes (about 3 lbs.)
2   small heads red oak lettuce, cleaned and dry
1   head frisée lettuce, cleaned and dry
½   head radicchio, cleaned and dry
1   Belgian endive, cleaned and dry
8   long fresh chives
1   bunch Enoki mushrooms, cleaned and dry

Garnish
¼   cup finely chopped red bell pepper
¼   cup finely chopped green bell pepper
¼   cup finely chopped scallions

Step 1.   To make the custard, preheat the oven to 325°F. Grease the inside of four small ceramic molds (about ½-cup size) with butter. (For a more decorative presentation, arrange one or two fresh herb leaves on the bottom of each mold.)

Step 2.   Whisk together the egg yolks, cornstarch, garlic and sugar in a bowl and set aside. Pour the half-and-half into a heavy saucepan and bring just to a simmer over low heat. (Do not boil.)

Step 3.   Whisk in the egg yolk mixture and then fold in the cheese until blended. Remove from the heat.

Step 4.   Ladle the mixture into the buttered molds. Set the molds in a roasting pan and place in the oven. Carefully, pour in enough hot water to come at least half way up the sides of the molds.

Step 5.   Bake for 12 to 15 minutes or until custard sets.

Step 6.   Remove molds from water bath and set aside.

Step 7.   To make vinaigrette, using a hand blender or whisk, combine the cilantro, garlic, vinegar, sugar, and salt and pepper to taste. Add the oil in a thin stream blending until combined. Set aside.

Step 8. To blanch tomatoes, score an "X" on the bottom of each tomato and place in a large pan of boiling water to blanch for 15 seconds. Remove tomatoes with a slotted spoon and plunge them into a bowl of ice water to loosen their skin. Then peel the tomatoes.

Step 9. To assemble, cut off a thin slice from the bottom of each tomato making them level. Then cut off enough of the tops so that you can scoop out and discard the pulp. Arrange each tomato on a serving plate.

Step 10. Twist off the stems from the red oak lettuce and cut off the stems of the frisée, radicchio and endive.

Step 11. Arrange 5 or 6 red oak leaves, one on top of the other but offset slightly. Stack a few leaves of frisée lettuce, radicchio and endive on top of the red oak. Carefully, roll up the lettuce layers (jellyroll-style) and place inside the tomato. Adjust the leaves until they flair creating the "bouquet" effect. Repeat with remaining tomatoes

Step 12. Insert a few Enoki mushrooms in the center of the greens, along with two fresh chives. Scatter some of the diced red and green peppers and a few scallions like confetti over each plate. Drizzle vinaigrette over the greens and the confetti.

Step 13. Place a custard on each plate to serve.

Yield: 4 servings (Pictured on page 52.)

MARINATED CALAMARI & PRAWN SALAD
WITH CAVIAR VINAIGRETTE

Vinaigrette
½ cup rice wine vinegar
1 tablespoon chopped fresh basil
Salt and pepper
1¼ cups extra virgin olive oil

16 medium shrimp, cleaned and deveined
1 to 2 tablespoons extra virgin olive oil

½ pound calamari (bodies only), cleaned
1 head red leaf lettuce (or a combination of the following: red leaf, curly endive, frisée or radicchio), cleaned and dry
4 teaspoons of caviar (choose any combination of the following: Tobiko, Sevruga, Oscietre or Salmon)

Step 1. To make vinaigrette, whisk together vinegar, basil, and salt and pepper to taste in a large bowl.

Step 2. Add oil in a thin stream and whisk until combined. Set aside with caviar.

Step 3. Season shrimp with salt and pepper to taste.

Step 4. Heat olive oil in heavy sauté pan over moderate heat. When oil is hot, add shrimp and sauté for 2 to 3 minutes or until pink. Remove from pan and set aside to cool.

Step 5. Blanch calamari in a pot of boiling salted water for just 20 to 30 seconds or until they begin to turn opaque. Remove from water with slotted spoon and rinse under cold water. Set aside to cool.

Step 6. Combine calamari and prawns with vinaigrette. Refrigerate for at least one hour.

Step 7. To assemble, arrange some lettuce leaves on each serving plate. Arrange some marinated seafood on each plate. Drizzle several teaspoons of the marinating liquid around edges of the plate and garnish with about 1 teaspoon caviar.

Yield: 4 to 6 servings (Pictured on page 50.)

BAKED SALMON & SCALLOP TERRINE

¼ cup Herb Mixture (page 64)

¾ cup chilled Panade (page 64)

1 tablespoon oil

¼ cup brandy

¼ cup dry white wine

½ pound salmon fillet

1 egg

1 teaspoon salt

½ teaspoon ground white pepper

1 to 2 teaspoons ground nutmeg

1¼ cups half-and-half

¼ pound scallops

Step 1. Prepare Herb Mixture, following the recipe on page 64. Prepare the Panade following the recipe on page 64.

Step 2. Heat oil in heavy, 10-inch sauté pan over medium heat. When oil is hot, add the ¼ cup herb mixture and sauté for 3 to 4 minutes. *Take pan off the flame.* Pour in the brandy, return pan to heat and deglaze for 1 to 2 minutes, loosening the cooked particles on the bottom of the pan. Remove from heat, stir in the wine and set aside to cool.

Step 3. Cut salmon into small strips. Place in a food processor fitted with a metal blade. Process for 1 to 2 minutes. Add the herb mixture and the egg and process until blended. Add the salt, white pepper, nutmeg and half-and-half and process until smooth. Chill the mixture (still in the food processor bowl) in the refrigerator for 1 to 2 hours.

Step 4. Meanwhile, lightly brush the side of a 4-cup terrine with oil and line it with plastic wrap, leaving enough excess to eventually fold over the top. Take care to press the plastic tightly into each corner. Preheat oven to 350° F.

Step 5. Position the bowl of salmon mixture back on the food processor. Add the chilled panade and process until well blended. Transfer mixture to a bowl. Cut scallops into quarters and fold into salmon mixture.

Step 6. Spoon the mixture into the lined terrine, smoothing the surface with a knife or offset spatula. Tap the terrine firmly against the counter a couple of times to remove any air bubbles. Fold over the excess plastic wrap to enclose top of terrine. (If the terrine does not have its own lid, cover the top with aluminum foil.)

Step 7. Set the terrine in a roasting pan and place in preheated oven. Pour in enough hot water to come three-fourths of the way up the sides of the terrine. Reduce oven temperature to 260°F and bake for 20 to 25 minutes or until the internal temperature of the terrine reaches 135°F.

Step 8. Remove and allow to reach room temperature. Unmold and cut into ¾-inch slices to serve.

Yield: 6 to 8 servings

CARROT, CAULIFLOWER & BROCCOLI
TERRINE WITH SAUCE VERTE

Sauce

2	tablespoons chopped watercress
2	tablespoons chopped fresh tarragon
2	tablespoons chopped parsley
2	tablespoons chopped spinach
2	egg yolks
1	teaspoon Dijon-style mustard
2	teaspoons lemon juice
½	teaspoon salt
2	teaspoons lemon juice
	Ground white pepper
1½	cups peanut oil or vegetable oil

Terrine

½	pound carrots, cleaned
½	pound cauliflower, trimmed
½	pound broccoli, trimmed
4	small shallots
1	clove garlic
1	tablespoon honey
½	teaspoon nutmeg
2¼	cups Basic Chicken Stock (page 31)
4	ounces plain (unflavored) gelatin
	Salt and white pepper
3	cups heavy cream

Step 1.   To make sauce, blanch the watercress, tarragon, parsley and spinach for about 30 seconds or until limp. Rinse under cold water, drain, and then squeeze completely dry in a clean towel. Set aside.

Step 2.   Whisk together egg yolks, mustard, lemon juice, salt and white pepper to taste in a small bowl until well blended. (Because you will be whisking vigorously, you may want to set the bowl on a folded towel to keep it from moving around as you work.)

Step 3.   Continue to whisk vigorously. Then slowly begin to add the oil, drop by drop at first, whisking as you go. As the oil is incorporated, increase to a slow steady stream of oil. When all of the oil is completely incorporated and the sauce (*mayonnaise*) has thickened, fold in the herbs and spinach until well combined. Cover and refrigerate until ready to use.

Step 4.   To make terrine, cut carrots, cauliflower and broccoli into large chunks. Chop the shallots and crush the garlic. Blanch vegetables separately in boiling water for 3 to 4 minutes or until tender. Drain thoroughly.

Step 5.   Place a heavy sauté pan over moderate heat. Add carrots, half the shallots and the honey. Cook for 3 to 4 minutes or until blended. Season to taste with salt and white pepper. Transfer to a bowl and set aside to cool.

Step 6.   Return pan to heat. Add the cauliflower and the remaining shallots. Cook for 3 to 4 minutes or until blended. Season to taste with salt and white pepper. Transfer to a second bowl and set aside to cool.

Step 7.   Return pan to heat. Add the broccoli, garlic and nutmeg. Cook for 3 to 4 minutes or until blended. Season to taste with salt and white pepper. Transfer to a third bowl and set aside to cool.

Step 8.   Using a food processor or hand blender, purée each vegetable separately until very smooth. You should have about two cups of each purée in three separate bowls.

Step 9.   Pour the stock into a double boiler. Sprinkle the surface with gelatin and allow it to bloom for about 10 minutes. Heat gelatin to a syrupy consistency over water that is 100° to 110°F. Whisk one-third of the gelatin mixture into each vegetable purée. Cover and chill for about 15 minutes (or place over an ice bath) until gelatin beings to set.

Step 10. Meanwhile, lightly brush the sides of a 6-cup terrine mold with oil and line it with plastic wrap. Preheat the oven to 300°F.

Step 11. Whip the cream to soft-peak stage. Spoon one-third of the cream into each purée, folding to combine. First, spoon the carrot mixture into the mold, smoothing the surface with a knife or an offset spatula. Repeat with the cauliflower layer and then broccoli layer.

Step 12. Tap the filled terrine firmly against the counter a couple of times to remove any air bubbles. Fold over the excess plastic wrap to enclose top of terrine.

Step 13. Place terrine in a roasting pan and set the pan in the oven. Carefully, pour in enough hot water to come at least half way up the sides of the terrine. (The water temperature should be around 170°F.) Bake for 25 to 30 minutes or until the internal temperature of the terrine reaches 135°F. Remove and allow to cool completely.

Step 14. Unwrap terrine and place on a cooling rack positioned over a cookie sheet. Pour gelatin evenly over the top of the terrine. Refrigerate for at least 3 hours. To serve, cut terrine into ¼-inch slices and serve with a dollop of sauce.

Yield: 8 to 10 servings (Pictured on page 51.)

VARIATION

Vegetable Terrine with Carrot & Mushroom Garnish: Prepare the above recipe as directed through Step 10. Whip the cream to a soft-peak stage. Fold half of the cream into each purée. Fold **½ cup blanched minced carrots** into the cauliflower mousse. Partially trim off stems from **10 to 12 whole mushrooms**. Then trim a little off *both sides* of each mushroom. Cook mushrooms in a little lemon juice for 2 to 3 minutes and cool. To assemble, spoon **broccoli mousse** into prepared terrine. Line up the trimmed mushrooms, side-by-side, down the center of the terrine, pressing them slightly into the mousse. Spoon **cauliflower mousse** on top. Complete by following Steps 12 through 14 above.

COUNTRY-STYLE PISTACHIO PATE
WITH MARINATED VEGETABLES & CORNICHONS

Herb Mix
2 yellow onions, peeled
4 to 5 cloves garlic, peeled
2 shallots
¼ cup olive oil
1 teaspoon chopped fresh thyme
1 tablespoon chopped fresh rosemary
1 tablespoon chopped parsley
1 tablespoon ground black pepper
1 ounce brandy
1 ounce dry sherry
2 ounces dry white wine

1 tablespoon olive oil

Panade
½ loaf white bread, crusts removed
3 egg yolks
1¼ cups half-and-half
1 tablespoon salt

Pâté
½ pound ground chicken
½ pound ground veal
½ pound ground pork
½ cup Herb Mix
1 cup Panade
1 egg
¼ cup brandy
1 cup heavy cream
1 tablespoon pâté spice mix (or combination of ground nutmeg, cinnamon, allspice, mace and ginger)
½ cup blanched pistachios, skins removed
1 tablespoon salt
1 teaspoon white pepper

Marinated Vegetables
1 cup red and/or yellow cherry tomatoes, halved
½ cup thinly sliced celery
½ cup thinly sliced radishes
10 to 12 cornichons, cut into thirds on a bias
1 tablespoon Balsamic vinegar
3 tablespoons light olive oil

Coarse Dijon-style mustard

Step 1. To make Herb Mix, chop the onions into medium (½-inch) dice. Mince the garlic and the shallots.

Step 2. Heat the olive oil in a heavy sauté pan over moderate heat. When oil is hot, add the onions garlic and shallots and sauté for 2 to 3 minutes until onions are translucent. Add the thyme, rosemary, parsley and black pepper, stirring to combine.

Step 3. *Take pan off the flame.* Pour in the brandy, sherry and wine. Return pan to moderate heat and deglaze for 1 to 2 minutes, loosening the cooked particles on the bottom of the pan.

Step 4. Cool slightly and then place in a food processor fitted with a metal blade. Process until smooth. Set aside to cool, then cover and store in refrigerator up to 3 days.

Step 5. To make Panade, cut the bread into large (1-inch) cubes and place in a bowl. Add the egg yolks, half-and-half and salt, mashing the mixture to a paste consistency. Cover and store in refrigerator up to 3 days. Makes about 4 cups.

Step 6. To make pâté, place half of the chicken, half of the veal and half of the pork into a food processor fitted with a metal blade. Add ½ cup Herb Mix and 1 cup Panade. Process for about 30 seconds to emulsify.

Step 7. With motor running, add the egg and brandy and continue to process until well mixed. Refrigerate mixture (still in processor bowl) and the remaining meats for about 1 hour.

Step 8. Meanwhile, lightly brush the inside of a 6-cup terrine with oil and line with plastic wrap, leaving enough excess to eventually fold over the top. Take care to press the plastic tightly into each corner. Preheat oven to 350°F.

Step 9. Place chilled meat mixture back on food processor. Process for about 30 seconds. With motor running, add the cream and pâté spice mix, and continue to blend until smooth.

Step 10. Transfer to a large bowl and fold in remaining meats and pistachios. Season with salt and white pepper to taste.

Step 11. Spoon mixture into the lined terrine, smoothing the surface. Tap the terrine firmly against the counter a couple of times to remove any air bubbles. Fold over the excess plastic wrap to enclose the top of terrine. (If terrine does not have its own lid, cover the top with aluminum foil.)

Step 12. Place in the preheated oven. Reduce temperature to 260°F and bake for 35 to 40 minutes or until internal temperature of the terrine reaches 160°F.

Step 13. Remove from the oven and allow to reach room temperature; then refrigerate for 1 to 2 hours.

Step 14. Meanwhile, to make marinated vegetables, combine the tomatoes, celery, radishes and cornichons. Add the vinegar, oil and salt and pepper to taste, stirring to combine. Refrigerate until ready to use.

Step 15. Carefully unmold pâté onto a serving platter and cut into ¼-inch-thick slices. Serve coarse Dijon-style mustard and marinated vegetables as accompaniments.

Yield: 8 to 10 servings (Pictured on page 49.)

TURKEY PATE
WITH CRANBERRY SAUCE

Pâté

1   small onion, peeled
2   stalks celery
¼   cup parsley
1   tablespoon vegetable oil
1   pound turkey breast meat
1   egg
¼   pound margarine

¼   pound Panade (page 64)
1   tablespoon pâté spice or Bells seasoning
1   teaspoon salt
1   teaspoon white pepper
1   small carrot, peeled
½   cup pistachio nuts, shelled

Purchased cranberry sauce (optional)

Step 1.   Chop the onion, celery and parsley into small (¼-inch) dice.

Step 2.   Heat oil in a heavy sauté pan over moderate heat. When oil is hot, add the onions and celery and sauté for 2 to 3 minutes or until onions are translucent. Stir in the parsley and set aside.

Step 3.   Cut the turkey into small (¼-inch) dice. Reserve 2 tablespoons for the garnish. Place remaining turkey meat in a food processor fitted with a metal blade. Process for 30 seconds. Then add egg, margarine, Panade, pâté spice, salt and white pepper to taste. Process until smooth and then transfer to a bowl.

Step 4.   Chop the carrot into small (¼-inch) dice. Blanch in boiling water for 2 to 3 minutes. Remove and drain. Blanch pistachios in boiling water for 2 to 3 minutes. Remove and place on a kitchen towel. Rub pistachios in the towel to remove their skins. Add the carrots and pistachios to the mixture, folding until blended.

Step 5.   Lightly brush the inside of a 4-cup terrine with oil and line with plastic wrap, leaving enough excess to eventually fold over the top. Take care to press the plastic tightly into each corner. Preheat oven to 350°F.

Step 6.   Spoon mixture into terrine, smoothing the surface. Tap the terrine firmly against the counter a couple of times to remove any air bubbles. Fold over the excess plastic wrap to enclose the top. (If terrine does not have its own lid, cover with foil.)

Step 7.   Place in the preheated oven. Reduce temperature to 260°F and bake for 35 to 40 minutes or until the internal temperature of the terrine reaches 140° to 150°F.

Step 8.   Remove from the oven and allow to reach room temperature, about 2 hours.

Step 9.   Remove from terrine, cut in ¼-inch-thick slices and serve with cranberry sauce.

Yield: 8 to 10 servings

BLACK BEAN SAUSAGE
WITH TOFU & FRESH CORN

2 small shallots
3 large cloves garlic
1 bunch fresh cilantro
¾ cup Basic Vegetable Stock (page 30)
2 ounces plain (unflavored) gelatin
1 tablespoon vegetable oil
2 cups cooked black beans
½ teaspoon salt
½ teaspoon ground white pepper

Garnish
½ medium green bell pepper
1 small carrot, peeled
¼ cup firm tofu
¼ cup fresh corn kernels

Plastic wrap
Butcher's twine (optional)

Step 1. Mince the shallots and garlic. Chop the cilantro. Set aside.

Step 2. Heat oil in a heavy sauté pan over moderate heat. When oil is hot, add the shallots and garlic. Sauté for 2 to 3 minutes or until tender. Set aside to cool.

Step 3. Place the beans, salt and white pepper in a food processor fitted with a metal blade and process until beans are puréed. Transfer to a large bowl.

Step 4. To make garnish, remove seeds and membrane from the bell pepper. Cut the pepper and carrot into very small (⅛-inch) dice.

Step 5. Heat oil in a sauté pan over moderate heat. When oil is hot, add pepper and carrots and sauté for 2 to 3 minutes or until tender. Cool completely.

Step 6. Drain and towel dry tofu. Cut the tofu into very small (⅛-inch) dice. Add tofu, corn, and cooled sautéed vegetables to the bean mixture, stirring to combine. Transfer to a bowl.

Step 7. Pour stock into a double boiler. Sprinkle the surface with gelatin and allow it to *bloom* for about 10 minutes. Heat gelatin to a syrupy consistency over water that is 100° to 110°F. Remove and allow gelatin to thicken slightly.

Step 8. Set the bowl of bean/vegetable mixture into a larger bowl filled with ice and stir occasionally as it cools. Add the gelatin, folding to combine, and continue stirring until thickened and well chilled.

Step 9. To assemble sausage, spoon mixture onto a sheet of plastic wrap in a long line. Roll up (like a cigar), twisting the ends closed and securing with butcher's twine, if desired. Chill for 3 to 4 hours or overnight.

Step 10. To serve, remove plastic and cut on the bias into ½-inch-thick slices.

Yield: 6 to 8 servings

CHICKEN & APPLE SAUSAGE
WITH LINGONBERRY SAUCE

Garnish

2   small leeks, cleaned
1   large Granny Smith apple
1   medium onion, peeled
¼   cup parsley leaves
2   tablespoon canola or vegetable oil
1   lemon
1   pound chicken leg meat

Farce (Forcemeat)

½   pound finely ground chicken breast
1   teaspoon salt
½   teaspoon ground white pepper
½   cup crushed ice

Pastry bag fitted with No. 4 tip
Pre-soaked sausage casings

¼   cup prepared mustard
¼   cup sour cream
2   cups lingonberry preserves

Step 1.   To make garnish, cut off most of the green portion of the leek and blanch in boiling salted water for 1 to 2 minutes until tender. Drain and squeeze out any excess moisture. Chop into small (¼-inch) dice.

Step 2.   Peel, core and chop apple into small (¼-inch) dice. Cut the onion into small (¼-inch) dice and chop the parsley.

Step 3.   Heat oil in a heavy sauté pan over moderate heat. When oil is hot, add the leeks, apples, onions and parsley. Sauté for 3 to 5 minutes until golden brown. Transfer the apple/vegetable garnish to a bowl and refrigerate.

Step 4.   To make farce, place the ground chicken, salt and white pepper in the bowl of a food processor fitted with a metal blade. Process for 30 seconds.

Step 5.   With motor running, drop in the crushed ice and continue to process for 1 to 2 minutes or until combined. (Crushed ice, a substitute for fat which is traditionally added at this point, will lighten the texture of the sausage.) Transfer the farce to a bowl and refrigerate.

Step 6.   To assemble sausage, cut the chicken leg meat into small (¼-inch) cubes. Remove zest from lemon in strips. (You should have 1 to 2 teaspoons.) Combine chilled farce, chilled apple/vegetable garnish and lemon zest in a large bowl. Add the cubed chicken meat, folding to combine.

Step 7.   Tie a knot at one end of the pre-soaked casing. Spoon mixture into a pastry bag fitted with a No. 8 plain tip. Pipe mixture into the casing and knot the other end.

Step 8.   Using your thumb and forefinger, squeeze the sausage every 3 or 4 inches to separate the mixture. Twist at those points to make individual sausage lengths. (See Step 9 of the sausage recipe on page 67 for making sausage using plastic wrap.)

Step 9.   Poach sausages in a pan of water (about 160°F) for 12 to 15 minutes. Remove, drain and transfer to a 350°F oven for 10 to 12 minutes or until browned. (Or, sauté over medium heat for 4 to 5 minutes or until browned.)

Step 10. Blend mustard and sour cream until smooth. Place a dollop of mustard sauce on individual plates (or, using a squeeze bottle, pipe mustard sauce in a decorative pattern across the center of the plate). Cut the sausages into thin, slanting slices and arrange on plate. Garnish with a spoonful of lingonberry preserves to serve.

Yield: About 4 servings

SEAFOOD SAUSAGE
WITH SAFFRON BEURRE BLANC

Farce (Forcemeat)

1	medium shallot, peeled
3	medium carrots, peeled
1	tablespoon fresh thyme
1	tablespoon vegetable oil
½	pound fresh halibut
¼	pound fresh scallops
1	pinch cayenne
¼	teaspoon white pepper
3	egg whites
½	cup crushed ice
¼	cup brandy
½	cup cream

Garnish

½	pound bay shrimp
½	pound salmon
1	teaspoon ground white pepper
1	teaspoon salt

Beurre Blanc

4	large shallots, peeled
¾	cup wine vinegar
1	cup Basic Fish Stock (page 32)
⅛	teaspoon saffron threads
¼	teaspoon white pepper
¾	cup cold unsalted butter, cut into small pieces

Pastry bag fitted with a No. 8 plain tip

Step 1. To make farce, mince the shallots, carrots and thyme. Heat oil in a heavy sauté pan over medium heat. When oil is hot, add shallots, carrots and thyme and sweat for 5 to 6 minutes. Set aside to cool.

Step 2. Meanwhile, cut halibut into pieces and slice the scallops in half. Place in a food processor fitted with a metal blade. Add the cooled shallots, cayenne and white pepper and process until smooth. Place in refrigerator (still in processor bowl) and chill for 1 hour.

Step 3. Remove from refrigerator, begin to process again while slowly adding egg whites, ¼ cup of the ice, brandy and the cream. Transfer mixture to a chilled bowl.

Step 4. To make garnish, cut the shrimp into pieces and cut the salmon into small (¼-inch) dice. Fold the shrimp, salmon, shallots, salt and pepper into the seafood farce.

Step 5. To assemble sausage, tie a knot at one end of the pre-soaked casing. Spoon mixture into a pastry bag fitted with a No. 8 plain tip. Pipe mixture into the casing and knot the other end.

Step 6. Using your thumb and forefinger, squeeze the sausage every 3 or 4 inches to separate the mixture. Twist at those points to make individual sausage lengths. (See Step 9 of the sausage recipe on page 67 for making sausage using plastic wrap.)

Step 7. Poach sausages in a pan of water (about 160°F) for 12 to 15 minutes.

Step 8. To make sauce, place the shallots, vinegar, and stock in a heavy, 1-quart saucepan over moderate heat. Cook for 3 to 5 minutes or until reduced by one-half. Add the white pepper and saffron. Remove pan from heat. Cut the butter into pieces and drop into sauce, a few at a time, whisking vigorously until smooth.

Step 9. Cut sausage on the bias into thin slices and serve sauce as an accompaniment.

Yield: 8 to 10 servings

CHICKEN IMPERIAL BALLOTINE

Marinade

1 small piece fresh ginger, peeled
½ bunch fresh thyme
1 tablespoon light soy sauce
1 tablespoon rice wine vinegar
2 boneless chicken breasts, halved

Filling

4 boneless chicken thighs
2 egg whites
½ teaspoon salt

1 cup half-and-half
8 to 10 asparagus, peeled
2 bunches fresh spinach, washed and dried
2 tablespoons butter
¼ teaspoon ground nutmeg

Maltaise Sauce

1 cup Hollandaise (page 42)
1 tablespoon orange juice
   (from blood orange, if possible)
½ teaspoon grated orange rind

Step 1. To make marinade, mince the ginger and thyme. Place in a bowl and add the soy sauce and rice wine vinegar, stirring to combine. Remove skin from chicken breasts, place in marinade, cover and marinate for 30 to 40 minutes.

Step 2. To make filling, cut the thigh meat into small pieces and place in a food processor fitted with a metal blade. Process for 30 seconds. With motor running, add the egg whites, salt and the half-and-half and continue to process just until smooth.

Step 3. Remove and transfer to a bowl. Chill in the refrigerator or position over a larger bowl filled with crushed ice until ready to assemble ballotine.

Step 4. Trim the asparagus to a length of about 6 inches. Blanch in boiling water for 2 to 3 minutes or until tender. Plunge into ice water to stop the cooking process, drain and set aside.

Step 5. Heat the butter in a heavy sauté pan over moderate heat. When butter is hot, add the spinach and sauté for 1 to 2 minutes. Season with nutmeg. Allow to cool slightly.

Step 6. To assemble, remove a chicken breast from the marinade and pat dry. Place in between two sheets of plastic wrap and pound to a thickness of ⅛-inch. Discard the top layer of plastic.

Step 7. Unfold and arrange a few pieces of spinach on each breast. Spread 2 to 3 tablespoons of chicken mixture evenly over the spinach. Place two asparagus spears in the center. Roll up each breast (like a cigar) and enclose in plastic wrap, twisting the ends to secure. Then wrap in aluminum foil. Repeat with remaining breasts.

Step 8.   Place in a pan filled with water over medium heat. Bring water temperature to about 170°F and poach for 10 to 12 minutes or until internal temperature reaches 135° to 140°F.

Step 9.   To make sauce, prepare Hollandaise according to directions on page 42. Add the orange juice and zest, folding to combine.

Step 10. Remove ballotines from the water, unwrap and allow to relax for 3 to 5 minutes. Spoon some sauce onto each plate. Cut ballotine into ½-inch-thick slices and arrange alongside.

Yield: About 4 servings

BASIC EGG PASTA
WITH VARIATIONS

14 ounces (3⅔ cups) all-purpose flour	½ teaspoon salt
7 ounces (1¾ cups) semolina	1 to 2 teaspoons extra virgin olive oil
5 large eggs, lightly beaten	Additional flour (for rolling out dough)

Step 1.   To make dough, combine flour and semolina on a large cutting board or work surface.

Step 2.   Form a well in the center of the flour and add the eggs, salt and oil.

Step 3.   Begin mixing with your fingers (of one hand), using the other hand to push flour from the outer edge of the well into the egg.

Step 4.   Continue mixing with one hand, using the other hand to support the outer edge (perimeter) of the flour well so as to prevent the batter from flowing out the side.

Step 5.   Continue mixing by hand until mixture becomes a firm paste. (At this point, you may need to adjust the consistency of the dough by adding a little water or additional all-purpose flour.)

Step 6.   Roll into a ball and knead, with the heel of your hand, for 5 to 10 minutes or until dough is smooth and feels silky.

Step 7.   Transfer to a bowl, cover with plastic and refrigerate for at least one hour.

Step 8.   Remove from the refrigerator and allow to rest at room temperature for 15 to 20 minutes before rolling out and cutting.

Step 9.   To finish pasta by hand, use a rolling pin to roll into a thin sheet (1/16-inch thick). Dust sheet lightly with flour and then roll up (like a cigar). Slice into desired thickness. Unroll each strip, shaking pasta to unravel.

Step 10.   To finish pasta using a machine, cut dough into four pieces. (Keep three of the pieces wrapped in plastic until ready to use.) Set the machine rollers so that they are opened to the widest setting. Flatten portion of dough, dust lightly with flour and pass it through the rollers.

Step 11.   Lay the rolled dough on a floured surface and fold in thirds to make three layers. Flatten again, lightly dust with more flour and pass through the machine, 5 to 6 more times, decreasing the settings of the rollers each time, until desired thickness is reached. Cut as described above, or cut dough using the machine attachment following manufacturer's directions.

Yield: 1½ pounds of dough

VARIATIONS

Beet-flavored Pasta: Add **1 to 2 tablespoons of beet purée**. Cook **1 medium peeled beet** until tender. Place in a food processor fitted with a metal blade and process until smooth. Press through a fine mesh strainer. Prepare pasta according to the recipe on opposite page.

Black Pasta: Add **1 teaspoon squid ink** (available at Asian markets or specialty shops). Prepare pasta according to the recipe on opposite page.

Saffron Pasta: Bloom **1 teaspoon turmeric or ⅛ teaspoon saffron threads in water**. Heat over moderate heat until reduced to 1 tablespoon; cool. Prepare pasta according to the recipe on opposite page, adding the liquid when incorporating the eggs.

SPINACH PASTA
WITH COLOR VARIATIONS

¾   **pound fresh spinach leaves**
14   **ounces (3⅔ cups) all-purpose flour**
7   **ounces (1¾ cups) semolina**

4   **large eggs, lightly beaten**
½   **teaspoon salt**
1   **to 2 teaspoons olive oil**

Step 1.   Blanch the spinach in boiling water for 15 to 20 seconds or just until wilted.

Step 2.   Remove spinach and plunge into a bowl of ice water to stop the cooking process.

Step 3.   Drain thoroughly. Then squeeze dry in a kitchen towel, taking care to remove as much moisture as possible. Place spinach in a food processor fitted with a metal blade and process until puréed.

Step 4.   Meanwhile, combine flour and semolina on a large cutting board or work surface. Form a well in the center of the flour and add the spinach, eggs, salt and oil.

Step 5.   Begin mixing with your fingers (of one hand), using the other hand to push flour from the outer edge of the well into the egg.

Step 6.   Continue mixing with one hand, using the other hand to support the outer edge (perimeter) of the flour well so as to prevent the batter from flowing out the side.

Step 7.   Continue mixing by hand until mixture becomes a firm paste. (At this point, you may need to adjust the consistency of the dough by adding a little water or additional all-purpose flour.)

Step 8.   Roll into a ball and knead, with the heel of your hand, for 5 to 10 minutes or until dough is smooth and feels silky.

Step 9.   Transfer to a bowl, cover with plastic and refrigerate for at least one hour.

Step 10.   Remove from the refrigerator and allow to rest at room temperature for 15 to 20 minutes before rolling out and cutting.

Step 11.   To finish pasta by hand, use a rolling pin to roll pasta into a thin sheet (1/16-inch thick). Dust sheet lightly with flour and then roll up (jellyroll-style). Slice into desired thickness. Unroll each strip, shaking pasta to unravel.

Step 12. To finish pasta using a machine, cut dough into four pieces. (Keep three of the pieces wrapped in plastic until ready to use.) Set the machine rollers so that they are opened to the widest setting. Flatten portion of dough, dust lightly with flour and pass it through the rollers.

Step 13. Lay the rolled dough on a floured surface and fold in thirds to make three layers. Flatten again, lightly dust with more flour and pass through the machine, 5 to 6 more times, decreasing the settings of the rollers each time, until desired thickness is reached. Cut as described above, or cut dough using the machine attachment following manufacturer's directions.

Yield: About 1½ pounds

VARIATIONS

Red Pepper Pasta: Substitute **2 tablespoons red bell pepper purée or pimento purée** for the spinach. Prepare pasta according to directions. **Yield: About 1½ pounds**

Pumpkin Pasta: Substitute **½ cup of pumpkin purée** (made from fresh cooked pumpkin) for the spinach. Prepare pasta according to directions. **Yield: About 1½ pounds**

LEMON DILL PASTA

3	lemons	5	eggs, lightly beaten
14	ounces (3⅔ cups) all-purpose flour	½	teaspoon salt
7	ounces (1¾ cups) semolina	1	to 2 teaspoons olive oil
2	tablespoons dried dill		

Step 1. Remove zest (colored portion only) from the lemons and finely chop. Squeeze the juice from one of the lemons–you should have 2 to 3 tablespoons–and set aside. (Reserve juice from two remaining lemons for other uses.)

Step 2. Combine flour, semolina and dill on a large cutting board or work surface. Form a well in the center of the flour and add the eggs, salt, oil, lemon juice and lemon zest.

Step 3. Begin mixing with your fingers (of one hand), using the other hand to push flour from the outer edge of the well into the egg.

Step 4. Continue mixing with one hand, using the other hand to support the outer edge (perimeter) of the flour well so as to prevent the batter from flowing out the side.

Step 5. Continue mixing by hand until mixture becomes a firm paste.

Step 6. Roll into a ball and knead, with the heel of your hand, for 5 to 10 minutes or until dough is smooth and feels silky.

Step 7. Transfer to a bowl, cover with plastic and refrigerate for at least one hour.

Step 8. Remove from the refrigerator and allow to rest at room temperature for 15 to 20 minutes before rolling out and cutting.

Step 9. To finish pasta by hand, use a rolling pin to roll pasta into a thin sheets (1/16-inch thick). Dust sheet lightly with flour and then roll up (like a cigar). Slice into desired thickness. Unroll each strip, shaking pasta to unravel.

Step 10. To finish pasta using a machine, cut dough into four pieces. (Keep three of the pieces wrapped in plastic until ready to use.) Set the machine rollers so that they are opened to the widest setting. Flatten portion of dough, dust lightly with flour and pass it through the rollers.

Step 11. Lay the rolled dough on a floured surface and fold in thirds to make three layers. Flatten again, lightly dust with more flour and pass through the machine, 5 to 6 more times, decreasing the settings of the rollers each time, until desired thickness is reached. Cut as described, or cut dough using the machine attachment following manufacturer's directions.

Yield: About 1½ pounds

WHOLE WHEAT PASTA

12 ounces (3 cups) whole wheat flour

9 ounces (2 cups) all-purpose flour

5 large eggs, lightly beaten

½ teaspoon salt

1 to 2 teaspoons olive oil

Step 1. Combine whole wheat flour and all-purpose flour on a large cutting board or work surface. Form a well in the center of the flour and add the eggs, salt, and oil.

Step 2. Begin mixing with your fingers (of one hand), using the other hand to push flour from the outer edge of the well into the egg.

Step 3. Continue mixing with one hand, using the other hand to support the outer edge (perimeter) of the flour well so as to prevent the batter from flowing out the side.

Step 4. Continue mixing by hand until mixture becomes a firm paste.

Step 5. Roll into a ball and knead, with the heel of your hand, for 10 to 12 minutes or until dough is smooth.

Step 6. Transfer to a bowl, cover with plastic and refrigerate for at least one hour.

Step 7. Remove from the refrigerator and allow to rest at room temperature for 15 to 20 minutes before rolling out and cutting.

Step 8. To finish pasta by hand, use a rolling pin to roll pasta into a thin sheet (1/16-inch thick). Dust sheet lightly with flour and then roll up (like a cigar). Slice into desired thickness. Unroll each strip, shaking pasta to unravel.

Step 9. To finish pasta using a machine, cut dough into four pieces. (Keep three of the pieces wrapped in plastic until ready to use.) Set the machine rollers so that they are opened to the widest setting. Flatten portion of dough, dust lightly with flour and pass it through the rollers.

Step 10. Lay the rolled dough on a floured surface and fold in thirds to make three layers. Flatten again, lightly dust with more flour and pass through the machine, 5 to 6 more times, decreasing the settings of the rollers each time, until desired thickness is reached. Cut as described above, or cut dough using the machine attachment following manufacturer's directions.

Yield: About 1½ pounds

SPINACH FETTUCINE ALFREDO

1 recipe Spinach Pasta (page 76)
2 cups freshly grated Parmesan cheese
4 tablespoons butter, at room temperature

¼ cup heavy cream, room temperature
Additional grated Parmesan cheese
(optional)

Step 1.   Prepare Spinach Pasta as directed on page 76. Roll out and cut into strips ⅜-inch wide and set aside to dry.

Step 2.   Bring 2 quarts of water to a full boil.

Step 3.   Drop in spinach pasta and stir. Cook for 2 to 3 minutes or until al dente.

Step 4.   Meanwhile, place the butter (in tablespoon-size lumps) in a large pasta bowl or serving platter.

Step 5.   Remove the cooked pasta using tongs or a pasta rake and place directly on top of the butter. Sprinkle grated cheese evenly over the top.

Step 6.   Pour the cream over the hot pasta and cheese, tossing to combine, until the pasta is coated on all sides with the sauce.

Step 7.   Serve with additional Parmesan cheese, if desired.

Yield: About 4 servings

BLACK PEPPER TAGLIATELLE
WITH SPRING VEGETABLE MELANGE

1   recipe Basic Egg Pasta (page 74)
¼   cup medium-grind black pepper

Dressing
1   large lemon
½   teaspoon salt
1   teaspoon red pepper flakes
1   teaspoon Dijon-style mustard
½   cup extra virgin olive oil
¼   teaspoon freshly ground black pepper

Vegetables
1   large zucchini
1   large yellow bell pepper
8   to 10 asparagus tips, trimmed
½   small head of cauliflower
½   cup fresh wild mushrooms (such as Chantrelles, oyster or morels)
½   cup red and yellow cherry tomatoes

Sprigs of fresh basil

Step 1:   Prepare Basic Egg Pasta as directed on page 74, adding the ground black pepper to the dry ingredients.

Step 2.   Roll out and cut into strips ¼-inch wide and set aside to dry as directed.

Step 3.   To make dressing, remove zest (color portion) from the lemon and mince finely. Squeeze out enough juice to make 3 tablespoons.

Step 4.   Whisk together the lemon zest, salt, red pepper flakes, mustard and lemon juice. Slowly whisk in oil, in a slow steady stream, until emulsified. Set aside.

Step 5.   Cut the zucchini into strips ¼-inch by ¼-inch by 2 inches long (called a *bâtonnet*). Cut off the top and bottom of the yellow pepper. Cut in half and remove the seeds. Flatten each half and remove the membrane. Cut into julienne strips. Cut the asparagus tips into small pieces. Slice the cauliflower and mushrooms.

Step 6.   Blanch the zucchini, yellow pepper, cauliflower and asparagus separately in boiling water for 1 to 3 minutes each or until tender but still crisp. Remove and plunge into ice water to stop the cooking process. Drain well and pat dry.

Step 7.   Heat the oil in a heavy sauté pan over moderate heat. When oil is hot, add the mushrooms and sauté for 2 to 3 minutes. Remove from oil and set aside.

Step 8.   Meanwhile, bring 2 quarts of water to a full boil. Drop in pasta and stir. Cook for 1 to 2 minutes or until al dente. Drain well; then transfer to a large bowl.

Step 9.   Combine dressing with cooked vegetables and gently toss with cooked pasta. Garnish with basil sprigs to serve.

Yield: 6 to 8 servings (Pictured on front cover and page 86.)

TRI-COLOR BAY SHRIMP RAVIOLI
WITH WHITE CLAM SAUCE

Filling

6   cloves garlic, peeled
16 to 18 leaves fresh basil leaves
1   pound bay shrimp, drained and squeezed
12 ounces goat cheese (or ricotta)
1   teaspoon ground black pepper

1   recipe Lemon Dill Pasta (page 78)
1   egg mixed with 2 tablespoons water

Clam Sauce

2   shallots, peeled
4   cloves garlic, peeled
1   tablespoon olive oil
¼   cup dry white wine
1   teaspoon dried oregano
½   teaspoon dried basil
¼   teaspoon cracked black pepper
¾   cup clam juice
1   pint half-and-half
6   ounces chopped (canned) clams
     Lemon juice

Step 1.   To make the filling, place the garlic, basil and shrimp in a mincer/chopper or small food processor and process until chopped. Transfer to a bowl and add the coat cheese and black pepper. Cover and chill in the refrigerator for about 30 minutes.

Step 2.   Meanwhile, to make the ravioli, roll out the dough into two sheets, as described on page 78, to a thickness of ¹⁄₁₆-inch. Lightly score the dough into rounds using a 3-inch cutter or a cup. Take care not to cut through the thickness of the dough. (These marks are important as they show you where to position the filling.)

Step 3.   Whisk together the egg and water (this is called an *egg wash*.)

Step 4.   Place one heaping tablespoon of the chilled filling in the center of each circle marked on the pasta. Brush the edges of the circle lightly with the egg wash.

Step 5.   Place a second sheet of pasta over the filling. Using your fingertips, press the pasta sheets together, working your fingers in and around the mounds of filling as you shape them. Take care to remove as much air as possible.

Step 6.   Cut each ravioli with a pastry wheel or knife. Crimp and seal the edges with a fork. Place each ravioli on a lightly floured cookie sheet, cover with a clean towel and refrigerate until ready to use.

Step 7.   To make sauce, chop the shallots and garlic.

Step 8. Heat the oil in a heavy sauté pan over moderate heat. When oil is hot, add the shallots and sauté for 1 to 2 minutes. Add the garlic and sauté for 1 to 2 minutes longer or until translucent.

Step 9. Take pan off the flame. Pour in the wine, return pan to heat and deglaze, loosening the cooked particles on the bottom of the pan. Add the oregano, basil and pepper and cook for 2 to 3 minutes or until mixture has reduced by one-half.

Step 10. Add the clam juice and cook for 4 to 5 minutes or until reduced by one-half. Add the half-and-half and cook for 6 to 8 minutes longer or until reduced by one-half. Keep sauce warm until ready to serve.

Step 11. To cook the ravioli, bring 2 quarts of water to a full boil. Drop in the raviolis, a few at a time, and cook for 4 to 6 minutes or until al dente.

Step 12. To serve, stir the chopped clams into the sauce until heated through. Place two raviolis on a plate and spoon over some clam sauce. Garnish with a sprig of fresh basil and grated Parmesan cheese.

Yield: 6 to 8 servings (Pictured on page 88.)

WHOLE WHEAT PAPPARDELLE
WITH PEAS & ANDOUILLE SAUSAGE

1	recipe Whole Wheat Pasta (page 79)	2	tablespoons olive oil
4	large tomatoes	¾	cup frozen peas, thawed
3	cloves garlic, peeled		Fresh basil leaves
1	pound Andouille sausage		Grated Parmesan cheese

Step 1. Prepare Whole Wheat Pasta as directed on page 79. Use a rolling pin to roll pasta into a thin sheet (1⁄16-inch thick). Dust sheet lightly with flour (to prevent pasta from sticking) and then roll up like a cigar. Slice into strips 1-inch wide. Unroll each strip, shaking pasta to unravel, and set aside until ready to cook.

Step 2. To blanch tomatoes, score an "X" on the bottom of each tomato and place in a large pan of boiling water to blanch for 15 seconds. Remove tomatoes with a slotted spoon and plunge them into a bowl of ice water to loosen their skin. Then peel the tomatoes, remove seeds and cut into medium (½-inch) dice.

Step 3. Chop the garlic and cut sausages into ¼-inch-thick slices.

Step 4. Heat a heavy, 10-inch sauté pan until hot over moderate heat. Add the sausages and cook, stirring occasionally, for 3 to 4 minutes or until lightly browned.

Step 5. Remove the sausages and pour off the fat. Return pan to heat and add the olive oil. When oil is hot, add the garlic and sauté for 1 to 2 minutes or until lightly browned.

Step 6. Return sausage to the pan and add peas and tomatoes. Reduce heat and simmer, uncovered, while you cook the pasta.

Step 7. Bring 2 quarts of water to a full boil. Drop in the pasta and stir. Cook for 3 to 4 minutes or until al dente. Drain well and toss with the sausage mixture until combined.

Step 8. To serve, stack the basil leaves on top of each other and roll up (like a cigar). Cut into very thin strips (called a *chiffonade*). Garnish top of pasta with basil and grated Parmesan cheese.

Yield: 4 to 6 servings

GRILLED VEGETABLE GAZPACHO WITH BLACK PEPPERCORN & ONION GARNISH

BLACK PEPPER TAGLIATELLE WITH
SPRING VEGETABLE MELANGE

CHESTNUT & CARROT SOUP WITH
CREME FRAICHE & CHERVIL

TRI-COLOR BAY SHRIMP RAVIOLI
WITH WHITE CLAM SAUCE

GINGERED PRAWNS IN BEAN SAUCE
WITH SPICY NOODLES

3   cloves garlic, peeled
1   small piece ginger, peeled
3   or 4 green scallions
½   pound broccoli
½   pound snow peas

Noodles
1   pound Chow Mein noodles
1   tablespoon sesame oil
1   tablespoon Chinese black bean chili sauce

¼   cup peanut oil
1   pound prawns, cleaned and deveined
¼   cup peanut sauce

Step 1.   Mince the garlic and the ginger. Cut the scallions on the bias into thin slices, about ⅛-inch long.

Step 2.   To prepare vegetables, cut and trim the broccoli into florets of equal size. Snap off the stems and pull any strings from the snow peas; cut into jullienne strips. Blanch the broccoli and the snow peas separately in boiling water. Plunge into ice water to stop the cooking process. Set aside.

Step 3.   To prepare noodles, bring two quarts of water to a full boil. Drop in the noodles and cook for 3 to 4 minutes until *al dente*. Drain well and toss with the sesame oil and chili sauce. Place on a warm serving platter.

Step 4.   Heat the peanut oil in a heavy, 10-inch sauté pan over moderate heat. When oil is hot, add the prawns and sauté for 1 minute.

Step 5.   Add garlic and ginger and sauté for 1 to 2 minutes longer. Add the broccoli and scallions, sauté for about 1 minute longer. Stir in the peanut sauce until heated.

Step 6.   To serve, spoon the prawns over the noodles and garnish with the blanched snow peas

Yield: 4 to 6 servings

CHICKEN IN OYSTER SAUCE
WITH RICE NOODLES

4 cloves garlic, peeled
1 large piece ginger, peeled
6 scallions, trimmed
2 boneless chicken breasts, halved and skin removed
¾ pound rice noodles
2 tablespoons sesame oil

3 to 4 tablespoons peanut oil
¼ cup oyster sauce
3 tablespoons soy sauce

Garnish
⅛ teaspoon black sesame seeds
Chopped fresh cilantro

Step 1. Mince the garlic and cut the scallions into pieces about 2-inches long. Mince most of the ginger, to make about ¼ cup. Coarsely grate the remaining ginger, to make about 1 teaspoon for the garnish.

Step 2. Cut the chicken into ¼-inch-thick strips.

Step 3. To prepare noodles, bring 2 quarts of water to a full boil. Drop in noodles and cook for 3 to 4 minutes or until al dente. Drain well and then toss with the sesame oil. Keep warm.

Step 4. Heat peanut oil in a heavy, 10-inch sauté pan. When oil is hot, add the chicken strips and sauté for 2 to 3 minutes or until lightly browned.

Step 5. Add the garlic, minced ginger and scallions. Continue to sauté for 2 to 3 minutes longer or until chicken is done. Stir in the oyster sauce and soy sauce until blended.

Step 6. Add noodles to the chicken mixture, tossing gently to combine, and transfer to a serving platter.

Step 7. To serve, garnish with the shredded ginger, black sesame seeds and cilantro.

Yield: 4 to 6 servings

GRILLED POLYNESIAN SHRIMP
WITH FRUIT KEBABS

8   bamboo skewers (8 to 10 inches long)

4   flat metal skewers (8 to 10 inches long)

20 large (14 to 16 count) shrimp

1   medium papaya

Marinade

1   small pineapple

1   large green bell pepper

½   small onion, peeled

¼   cup cider vinegar

¼   cup brown sugar

2   tablespoons tomato sauce

Garnish

Cooked cellophane noodles

1   teaspoon black sesame seeds

Step 1.   To prevent bamboo skewers from burning, pre-soak them in water for about 2 hours prior to grilling.

Step 2.   Peel and devein the shrimp, leaving the tails intact, if desired. Set aside.

Step 3.   To make marinade, slice off the top and bottom of the pineapple. Cut into quarters, then into eighths. Remove the tough core from each section. Cut into 1½-inch pieces. Transfer half of the pineapple to the bowl of a food processor fitted with a metal blade. Set the other half aside.

Step 4.   Cut off the top and bottom of the green pepper. Cut in half and remove the seeds. Flatten each half and remove the membrane. Cut into 1½-inch pieces. Transfer half of the pepper to the bowl of the food processor and set the other half aside. Cut the papaya in half lengthwise. Remove and discard seeds. Then cut each half into quarters. Cut sections into 1½-inch pieces and set aside.

Step 5.   Coarsely chop the onion and place in the food processor bowl containing the pineapple and pepper. Process for about 1 minute or until coarsely chopped, taking care not to liquify the fruit/vegetable mixture.

Step 6.   Combine the vinegar, brown sugar and tomato paste in a large bowl. Add the puréed fruit/vegetable mixture and stir to combine. Set aside.

Step 7.   Working on a flat surface, lay five shrimp in a row, one right next to the other, so that all the tails go in the same direction.

Step 8. Using one hand to hold the shrimp in position, thread a pre-soaked bamboo skewer through the center of each shrimp. Thread a second skewer, parallel and just to one side of the first skewer, through the shrimp. (Double-skewered shrimp are much easier to turn over when cooked on a grill.)

Step 9. Place the skewered shrimp in a shallow pan and pour over the marinade. Cover and marinate for no more than 1 hour.

Step 10. Meanwhile, using the flat metal skewers, thread the reserved pieces of pepper, papaya and pineapple onto the skewers.

Step 11. Preheat the grill, according to manufacturer's directions, and lightly season with vegetable oil. The temperature should be medium.

Step 12. Remove skewered shrimp from marinade (reserve marinade). Place skewers over medium heat and grill for 3 to 4 minutes. Turn skewers over and cook for 3 to 4 minutes longer or until shrimp turn pink. As soon as you turn over the shrimp, place the fruit skewers on the grill. They should take no more than 3 to 4 minutes to heat completely.

Step 13. Remove shrimp and fruit from grill and arrange on platter of cooked cellophane noodles. To serve, garnish with a sprinkling of black sesame seeds.

Yield: 4 servings

GRILLED PRAWNS
WITH QUINOA

8 bamboo skewers (8 to 10 inches long)	20 large (14 to 16 count) prawns, in their shells

Marinade

3 slices bacon	*Quinoa*
½ small onion, peeled	2 tablespoons peanut oil
1 tablespoon dry mustard	1 small onion, peeled
2 tablespoons chile sauce	2 tablespoons roasted pumpkin seeds
2 to 3 tablespoons fresh lemon juice	2 tablespoons dried papaya
½ teaspoon celery seed	1 cup quinoa
	1¾ cups Basic Chicken Stock (see page 31)
	¾ teaspoon salt

Step 1.   To prevent bamboo skewers from burning, pre-soak them in water for about 2 hours .

Step 2.   To make marinade, cut the bacon into medium (½-inch) dice. Finely mince the onion and set aside. Heat sauté pan over moderate heat. When pan is hot, add the bacon and sauté for 2 to 3 minutes or until lightly browned. Add the onion, dry mustard and chile sauce. Reduce heat and cook, stirring occasionally, for 3 to 5 minutes or until onion is translucent. Add the lemon juice and celery seed and continue to cook for 1 to 2 minutes longer.

Step 3.   Remove from heat, cool slightly and transfer to a wide dish or baking pan. Arrange the prawns in the marinade, turning to coat all sides evenly, and marinate for no more than 1 hour.

Step 4.   To make quinoa, cut the onion into small (¼-inch) dice. Heat the oil in a heavy, 1-quart sauce pan. Sauté the onions and the seeds for 1 to 2 minutes or until tender. Add dried fruit and quinoa and mix well. Add stock, salt and pepper and stir to mix. Bring to a boil, cover and reduce heat, boiling gently for 15 to 18 minutes or until tender and fluffy.

Step 5.   Preheat the grill, according to manufacturer's directions, and lightly season with vegetable oil. The temperatue of the grill should be medium. Remove prawns from marinade. Lay five prawns in a row, one right next to the other, so that all the tails go in the same direction. Using one hand to hold the prawns in position, thread a pre-soaked bamboo skewer through the center of each prawn. Thread a second skewer, parallel and just to one side of the first skewer, through the prawns.

Step 6.   Place skewers over medium heat and grill, turning once and basting with reserved marinade, for 3 to 4 minutes per side or until shrimp turn pink. Arrange skewers over the quinoa to serve.

Yield: 4 servings

DEVILED CRAB CAKES IN SHELLS
WITH REMOULADE SAUCE

Sauce

2 cups mayonnaise
2 teaspoons dry mustard
3 cloves garlic, peeled
3 or 4 gherkins
2 tablespoons capers, drained
2 tablespoons parsley
1 tablespoon fresh tarragon leaves
½ teaspoon anchovy paste

Cakes

1 large green bell pepper
1 medium onion, peeled

2 stalks celery
2 cloves garlic, peeled
3 tablespoons canola oil
¼ teaspoon cayenne pepper
½ teaspoon dry mustard
½ teaspoon paprika
½ cup Béchamel Sauce (page 35)
1 pound crabmeat, flaked
1½ cups fresh French breadcrumbs

1 cup safflower oil
2 tablespoons minced parsley

Step 1. To make sauce, mince the gherkins, capers, parsley and tarragon. Place in a bowl and add the mayonnaise, mustard, garlic, gherkins, capers, parsley, tarragon and anchovy paste. Cover and chill.

Step 2. Cut off the top and bottom of the green pepper. Cut in half and remove seeds. Flatten each half and remove the membrane; then cut into very small (⅛-inch) dice. Finely chop the onion and celery and then mince the garlic.

Step 3. Heat the 3 tablespoons of canola oil in a heavy, 2-quart saucepan over moderate heat. When oil is hot, add the pepper, onion and celery and sauté for 2 to 3 minutes or until onion is translucent. Stir in the cayenne, mustard and paprika. Then add the Béchamel, crabmeat and one-half of the breadcrumbs, mixing to combine.

Step 4. Remove pan from the heat and slowly add more breadcrumbs–just enough to form a dough-like consistency. (Reserve enough crumbs to press into the cakes just prior to pan frying.) Scoop up about two heaping tablespoons of crab mixture and using your hands, shape into a 2-inch round crab cake, about ½-inch thick. Repeat procedure with remaining crab mixture. (If crab shells are available, you can place some of the mixture in the top portion of each shell.)

Step 6. Heat ½-inch of safflower oil in a heavy, deep-sided skillet over medium heat to a temperature of 375°F. Lower the crab cakes (or stuffed shells) into the hot oil and fry, uncovered and maintaining a temperature of 375°F, for about 2 minutes per side (turning once).

Step 7. Remove with a slotted spoon and place on a paper towel to drain. Arrange crab cakes on serving platter, garnish with minced parsley and serve with sauce as an accompaniment.

Yield: 6 to 8 servings

CORN & CLAM FRITTERS
WITH CAJUN MAYONNAISE

Mayonnaise

⅛ cup capers, drained

5 or 6 cornichons

½ small onion, peeled

1 cup Basic Mayonnaise (page 43)

2 tablespoons fresh lemon juice

2 tablespoons tarragon vinegar

1 tablespoon Dijon-style mustard

2 teaspoons Cajun spices

3 tablespoons chopped parsley, chervil or tarragon

Fritters

1 cup bread flour

½ teaspoon salt

2 tablespoons granulated sugar

2 eggs

1 cup beer

6 ounces chopped (canned) clams, drained

½ cup fresh corn, hulled

½ teaspoon onion powder

½ teaspoon lemon pepper

1 clove garlic, peeled

¼ cup parsley

Corn oil

Step 1.   Prepare Basic Mayonnaise following directions on page 43.

Step 2.   Finely chop the capers, cornichons and the onion. Place in a bowl and add the mayonnaise, lemon juice, vinegar, mustard, Cajun spices and herbs. Mix well. (If you like a spicy flavor, add additional Cajun spice.) Cover and chill for one hour.

Step 3.   To make fritters, sift together the flour, salt and sugar.

Step 4.   Separate the eggs, placing the whites in a clean bowl large enough for whipping. (Do not whip egg whites.) Place the yolks in a very large bowl and add the beer, mixing with a hand blender or whisk until combined.

Step 5.   Gradually stir in the flour mixture, blending until smooth. Refrigerate for about 30 minutes. Meanwhile, mince the garlic and finely chop the parsley.

Step 6.   Remove batter from the refrigerator and stir in the clams, corn, onion powder, lemon pepper, garlic and parsley.

Step 7.   Whip the egg whites to a stiff-peak stage and fold into the chilled clam mixture, making a dough-like batter.

Step 8.   Heat ½-inch of safflower oil in a heavy, deep-sided skillet over medium heat to a temperature of 375°F. Using a spoon, scoop up about 2 tablespoons of batter and drop into the oil. Repeat procedure, taking care not to put too many fritters in the oil at once. (This will cause the oil temperature to drop and the fritters will become heavy).

Step 9.   Fry, uncovered while maintaining a temperature of 375°F, for about 2 minutes per side (turning once) or until golden brown. Remove with a slotted spoon and place on paper towels to drain.

Step 10. Arrange fritters on a serving platter and offer Cajun mayonnaise as an accompaniment.

Yield: 4 to 6 servings

SAUTEED SNAPPER FRANCISCAN
WITH LEEKS

2   or 3 small leeks, washed and trimmed
4   snapper fillets (6 oz. each),
    with skin on
4   to 6 tablespoons olive oil
1   cup fine sourdough breadcrumbs
8   cloves elephant garlic, peeled

16 to 20 marinated artichoke hearts,
    well drained
⅔   cup dry Chardonnay
½   cup tomato relish
    (page 114), optional

Step 1.   Trim off most of the green from the leeks and split the white portion in half lengthwise. Cut the halves into julienne strips.

Step 2.   Brush both sides of the snapper with a little oil and then press in the breadcrumbs until both sides are well covered.

Step 3.   Heat 2 tablespoons of the olive oil in a heavy sauté pan over moderate heat. When oil is hot, add the leeks and sauté for 1 to 2 minutes or until tender. Remove and keep warm in the oven.

Step 4 .   Reheat pan over moderate heat, adding 1 or 2 additional tablespoons of olive oil as needed. When oil is hot, add the snapper fillets, skin-side down, and sauté for 2 to 3 minutes per side (turning once) or until fish "sets" and is slightly springy to the touch. Remove and keep warm in the oven.

Step 5.   Heat remaining tablespoon of oil in another sauté pan over moderate heat. When oil is hot, add the garlic and sauté for 2 to 3 minutes. Add the drained artichokes and sauté for 1 minute longer.

Step 6.   Take pan off the flame. Pour in the wine, return pan to moderate heat and deglaze for 1 to 2 minutes, loosening the cooked particles on the bottom.

Step 7.   Place sautéed leeks in center of each plate and arrange a piece of snapper, skin-side-up, on top. Spoon over some artichokes, garlic and sauce. Garnish each fillet with a spoonful of tomato relish, if desired.

Yield: 4 servings

SAUTEED SNAPPER GALICIAN
WITH BLACK BEANS, TOMATOES & OLIVES

1	medium onion, peeled	4	tablespoons olive oil
2	cloves garlic, peeled	¼	cup Basic Fish Stock (page 32)
2	small tomatoes	2	cups cooked black beans
24	to 30 pitted Spanish olives	¼	cup fresh lemon juice
4	boneless snapper fillets (6 oz. each), skin removed	2	tablespoons chopped parsley
4	tablespoons Spanish paprika		Extra whole Spanish olives (optional)

Step 1.   Cut the onion into small (¼-inch) dice. Mince the garlic and chop the tomatoes into medium (½-inch) dice. Slice the olives in half.

Step 2.   Dust one side of each snapper fillet with paprika.

Step 3.   Heat the olive oil in a heavy, 10-inch sauté pan over moderate heat. When oil is hot, add the snapper, paprika-side-down, and sauté for 2 to 3 minutes per side (turning once) or until fish sets and is slightly springy to the touch.

Step 4.   Remove from the pan and keep warm in the oven.

Step 5.   Return pan to heat. When hot, add the onion and sauté for 2 to 3 minutes or until until translucent. Add garlic and sauté for 1 to 2 minutes longer. Stir in the olives and tomatoes and cook for 1 to 2 minutes.

Step 6.   *Take pan off the flame.* Pour in the stock, return pan to moderate heat and deglaze for 1 to 2 minutes, loosening the cooked particles on the bottom.

Step 7.   Stir in the beans, lemon juice and chopped parsley. Cook, stirring to combine, for 1 to 2 minutes longer or until heated through.

Step 8.   To serve, spoon the bean/olive mixture onto a serving platter and arrange snapper fillets on top. Garnish with a few whole olives, if desired.

Yield: 4 servings   (Pictured on page 105.)

GRILLED CALIFORNIA HALIBUT
WITH INFUSED SHRIMP OIL

Shrimp Oil
1   carrot, peeled
1   small onion, peeled
2   stalks celery
¼   pound shrimp (20 to 24 count), with shells
½   cup peanut oil
1   sprig tarragon
¼   teaspoon cayenne
½   cup dry white wine
1   tablespoon tomato paste
1   cup Basic Fish Stock (page 32)
½   cup safflower oil

Fish
2   tablespoons olive oil
4   halibut fillets (6 oz. each), cut ½-inch thick
1   cup fine sourdough breadcrumbs
1   pound asparagus
1   small red bell pepper

Garnishes (optional)
1   parsnip, peeled
8   to 10 large fresh basil leaves
1   cup hot mashed potatoes
1   cup freshly-cooked corn

Additional safflower oil

Step 1.   To prepare Shrimp Oil, cut the carrot, onion and celery into small (¼-inch) dice. Coarsely chop the shrimp (with shells still on) and set aside.

Step 2.   Heat 2 tablespoons peanut oil in a heavy, 3-quart saucepan over moderate heat. When oil is hot, add the onions and sauté for 1 to 2 minutes. Add the carrots and celery and sauté for 1 to 2 minutes longer.

Step 3.   Add the chopped shrimp, tarragon and cayenne pepper to the vegetables and sear 2 to 3 minutes or until the shrimp are done and turn pink.

Step 4.   Take pan off the flame. Pour in the wine, return pan to moderate heat and deglaze for 1 to 2 minutes, loosening the cooked particles on the bottom, or until reduced so that pan is almost dry. Add the tomato paste, stirring to combine.

Step 5.   Pour in the fish stock, reduce heat and simmer, uncovered, for 20 to 30 minutes. Remove from the heat, pour into a strainer or china cap lined with several layers of cheesecloth and cool. (To speed up the cooling process, place the bowl in an ice bath.)

Step 6.   Whisk in the safflower oil, in a slow continuous stream, until combined. If not using right away, cover and refrigerate. (This may be refrigerated for up to 3 months.)

Step 7. To prepare garnishes, thinly slice the parsnip lengthwise (from top to bottom) using a vegetable peeler. Wash the basil leaves and pat dry thoroughly .

Step 8. Heat ¼ inch of safflower oil in a heavy sauté pan over medium heat to a temperature of 325°F. When oil is hot, drop in the parsnip slices and fry for 3 to 4 minutes or until crisp. Remove and drain on paper towels.

Step 9. Bring oil back to a temperature of 325°F. Drop in individual basil leaves and fry for about 1 minute or until crispy. Remove and drain on paper towels.

Step 10. To prepare vegetables, cut off the ends of the asparagus and peel outer edge of the stems, leaving a little of the greens. Cut the red pepper in half and remove the seeds. Flatten each half and trim away the inside membrane. Then cut into julienne strips and set aside.

Step 11. To prepare halibut, pat halibut fillets dry and dip both sides into olive oil. Press in breadcrumbs evenly on both sides. Preheat broiler (or preheat grill according to manufacturer's instructions). The temperature should be moderately hot.

Step 12. Heat the olive oil in a heavy sauté pan over moderate heat. When oil is hot, add the asparagus and red pepper and sauté for 2 to 3 minutes or until tender but still crisp. Cover and keep warm.

Step 13. Place the halibut fillets under the broiler (or on the hot grill) and grill for 2 to 3 minutes per side, turning once, or until fish sets and is slightly springy to the touch.

Step 14. Place a few hot asparagus spears on the center of a plate. Arrange 3 or 4 red pepper strips over the asparagus followed by a piece of halibut.

Step 15. Place the grilled halibut over the vegetables on an angle.

Step 16. If using optional garnishes, place a dollop (or pipe a rosette) of hot mashed potatoes on each side of the plate. Place a fried basil leaf into one of the rosettes and a fried parsnip into the other.

Step 17. Sprinkle corn like confetti over the halibut and decorate outer edge of each plate with a line of infused shrimp oil.

Yield: 6 servings

SEABASS EN PAPILLOTE
WITH BASIL BUTTER

Compound Butter
2 cloves garlic, peeled
½ bunch fresh basil leaves
8 ounces butter, room temperature
1 to 2 teaspoons fresh lemon juice
⅛ cup crushed ice
Parchment paper

Vegetables
8 small redskinned potatoes, tournade

1 large leek, cleaned
½ fennel bulb, trimmed
1 medium red bell pepper

4 pieces of parchment paper, cut into 12-inch squares
4 tablespoons clarified butter
4 boneless seabass fillets (6 oz. each), with skin

Step 1. To prepare butter, mince the garlic and finely chop the basil leaves. Whip the butter until smooth. Then add the garlic, basil, lemon juice and crushed ice. Continue to whip vigorously for 2 to 3 minutes or until ice is well incorporated.

Step 2. Place the mixture on a sheet of parchment paper and roll into 1-inch-thick cylinder. Refrigerate for at least one hour or until butter is firmly set.

Step 3. To prepare vegetables, trim the potatoes in football-shaped pieces about 1-inch long by ½-inch wide. This is called *tourner*. Cook in boiling water for 5 to 6 minutes or until three-quarter doneness. Plunge into ice water to stop the cooking process. Drain and set aside.

Step 4. Trim the leek and cut into fine julienne strips; set aside. Remove outer tough portion of fennel bulb and cut into fine julienne strips; set aside.

Step 5. Cut off the top and bottom of the red pepper. Cut in half and remove the seeds. Flatten each half, remove the membrane and cut into fine julienne strips. Set aside.

Step 6. To assemble, fold each piece of parchment paper in half. (You will eventually be making something shaped like an envelope.) Open up the parchment and brush with some clarified butter. Arrange the leeks, fennel and red pepper strips on the buttered parchment near the fold.

Step 7. Preheat oven to 425°F. Position the rack in the lower third of the oven.

Step 8. Place the seabass on top of the vegetables, skin side facing up.

Step 9. Cut off two ¼-inch-thick slices of basil butter and place on fish. Tuck two potatoes around the edge of fish.

Step 10. Fold the paper back down over the fish and vegetables. To seal the "parchment envelope", pleat and fold each of the three open sides, rounding the corners as you go, until the envelope is shaped like a half-moon. Repeat procedure by folding the edges over again. Be sure the entire length of the curved edge is sealed well as this seal locks in the moisture and flavor as well as traps air allowing the parchment to puff up as it cooks.

Step 11. Repeat with remaining parchment, fish and vegetables. Place the four envelopes on a sheet pan and bake in the preheated oven for 10 to 12 minutes. The envelopes will puff up to double their size and the paper will brown slightly .

Step 12. Remove from the oven and place on individual plates. To serve, carefully split the top of the paper with a knife (or pair of scissors) and fold the paper back exposing the fish and vegetables.

Yield: 4 servings

CHINESE STEAMED FISH
WITH HOT SESAME OIL

1	small piece of ginger, peeled	4	fish steaks or fillets (6 oz. each), such as seabass
3	cloves garlic, peeled	¼	cup sesame oil
6	scallions	2	tablespoons oyster sauce
2	pieces lemon grass		Fresh cilantro leaves (optional)
½	small head Chinese cabbage or lettuce		

Step 1.   Cut the ginger into thin strips (to make about ½ teaspoon). Thinly slice the garlic and cut scallions on a bias into ¼-inch pieces.

Step 2.   Cut the lemon grass into pieces about 2 to 3 inches long.

Step 3.   Place a wok (or wide pan) partially filled with water on the burner and drop in the pieces of lemon grass. Bring to a simmer over medium-low heat.

Step 4.   Meanwhile, line the bottom of a Chinese bamboo steamer with cabbage leaves.

Step 5.   To prepare fish, make several slashes on both sides of the fish, about ¼-inch deep, and arrange in the lined steamer. Sprinkle fish with ginger strips and garlic.

Step 6.   Place cover on steamer basket and position in wok over simmering water. Steam for 12 to 15 minutes or until fish is set and is slightly springy to the touch.

Step 7.   Meanwhile, heat the sesame oil in a small, heavy saucepan over moderate heat.

Step 8.   To serve, pour the oyster sauce onto a large platter. Lift fish from steamer and place over the oyster sauce. Immediately, pour over the hot sesame oil. Garnish with a sprinkling of scallions and cilantro, if desired.

Yield: 4 servings

SAUTEED SNAPPER GALICIAN WITH
BLACK BEANS, TOMATOES & OLIVES

PORK TENDERLOIN WITH RHUBARB SAUCE, APPLE-MINT RELISH & SWEET POTATO HAY

GRILLED TUSCAN CHICKEN BREAST WITH POLENTA & MEDITERRANEAN VEGETABLES

POACHED BEEF TENDERLOIN WITH
SABAYON & WILD MUSHROOM SAUTE

POACHED WHOLE SALMON
WITH FRESH DILL & TARRAGON

Poaching Liquid

1 bunch fresh dill
1 bunch fresh tarragon
2 cloves garlic, peeled
1 small onion, peeled
1 quart water
½ cup dry white wine
1 bay leaf

1 tablespoon whole black peppercorns
2 tablespoons fresh lemon juice

1 piece salmon (about 3 lbs.), cleaned and scaled

Butcher's twine
Lemon wedges

Step 1. To make poaching liquid, remove sprigs of dill from their stems. Place stems in a 5-quart fish poacher and reserve dill sprigs for garnish. Remove tarragon leaves from their stems. Place stems in fish poacher and reserve leaves for garnish.

Step 2. Mince the garlic and thinly slice the onion and place each in the fish poacher along with the water, wine, bay leaf, peppercorns and lemon juice.

Step 3. Bring to boil over moderate heat. Reduce heat to low or enough so that the liquid is simmering (80°F) but not boiling.

Step 4. Meanwhile, shape the salmon into a roast by tucking under the edges. Holding one end of a long piece of butcher's twine, slip it under the entire length of the roast. Bring up the end and loosely tie a knot. Loop the long end of the remaining twine over your wrist. Expand the loop large enough to fit over the roast. Slide the loop over the roast and secure, about an inch from the previous knot, by pulling the long end of the string hard enough to tighten the loop. Take care to keep each loop equally taut. Repeat every inch until entire roast has been laced. Secure with a knot.

Step 5. Place salmon roast on the poaching rack and lower into the liquid.

Step 6. Cover and poach for 8 to 12 minutes. Then, turn off the heat and allow salmon to sit with the cover on for another 10 minutes to finish cooking.

Step 7. Lift out the rack. Remove salmon and arrange on a serving platter. Garnish with the reserved dill sprigs and tarragon leaves. Offer wedges of lemon alongside.

Yield: 4 to 6 servings

GRILLED MOROCCAN CHICKEN

Infused Oil

½   cup olive oil
4   to 6 cloves garlic, peeled

Marinade

2   cloves garlic, peeled
2   teaspoons fresh cilantro
¼   medium red onion, peeled
¼   cup fresh lemon juice
¼   cup olive oil
½   teaspoon paprika
1   dried chile pepper, crushed
½   teaspoon ground cumin (dry-roasted,
    if desired)
1   tablespoon ground turmeric
1   teaspoon Kosher salt
¼   cup golden raisins
    Pinch sugar

4   boneless chicken breasts, halved
    and skin removed

Skewered Vegetables

2   zucchini
2   small red onions, peeled
2   yellow summer squash
2   Japanese eggplants
2   green bell peppers

    Vegetable oil

2   large tomatoes, cut into wedges
4   cups prepared tabbouleh or rice
    (optional)

Step 1.   To make garlic oil, heat the olive oil in a heavy, 1-quart saucepan over medium heat. Crush (or mince) the garlic. When oil is hot, add the garlic. Remove pan from heat and allow to steep until completely cooled. Pour through a fine strainer. (Oil may be stored in an airtight container for up to 1 month.)

Step 2.   To make marinade, coarsely chop the red onion. Place it in the bowl of a food processor fitted with a metal blade along with the garlic, cilantro, lemon juice, olive oil, paprika, chile pepper, cumin, turmeric, salt, raisins and sugar. Process into a smooth paste.

Step 3.   Arrange the chicken breasts in a shallow baking pan. Pour over the marinade, turning the chicken to coat all sides. Cover and refrigerate for 1 to 2 hours. (If the chicken is not fully submerged in the marinade, turn the breasts over again after 1 hour.)

Step 4.   To prepare vegetables, trim ends off of zucchini and cut each into 2-inch pieces. Cut the onions in half and cut the squash and eggplant into quarters.

Step 5. Cut off the top and bottom of the green peppers. Cut in half and remove the seeds. Flatten each half, remove the membrane and 2-inch pieces. Thread all the vegetables onto flat metal skewers. (The order is unimportant because once grilled, the vegetables will be removed.)

Step 6. Preheat the grill, according to manufacturer's directions, and lightly season with vegetable oil. The temperature of the grill should be moderately hot.

Step 7. Arrange the skewered vegetables over moderate heat and grill, turning as needed and basting with the garlic oil, for 3 to 4 minutes or until vegetables are cooked. Remove and set aside to cool slightly.

Step 8. Season the grill again with vegetable oil. Remove chicken from marinade, shaking off excess, and place over medium heat. Grill for 3 to 5 minutes per side, turning once and basting with reserved marinade.

Step 9. Meanwhile, spoon tabbouleh onto a warm serving platter. Arrange chicken on top. Remove vegetables from skewers and arrange alongside. Garnish platter with tomato wedges.

Yield: 8 servings

GRILLED TUSCAN CHICKEN BREAST
WITH POLENTA & MEDITERRANEAN VEGETABLES

Polenta
6   cups water
2   cups polenta
2   to 3 teaspoons salt
2   to 4 tablespoons butter

Marinade
1   small fennel bulb, trimmed
1   small white onion, peeled
1   tablespoon lemon zest
2   teaspoons fresh rosemary
2   tablespoons Italian parsley
1   teaspoon fresh thyme leaves
2   tablespoons balsamic vinegar
1   cup olive oil

2   boneless chicken breasts, halved
    and skin removed

Vegetables
2   small fennel bulbs
2   large tomatoes
8   to 12 asparagus
8   to 12 cooked baby artichokes (optional)
    Salt and ground black pepper

1   tablespoon olive oil or vegetable oil
    Extra sprigs of fresh thyme

Step 1.   To make polenta, bring the water to a full boil in a heavy, 3-quart saucepan over moderate heat. Add the salt. Slowly, pour in the polenta in a continuous stream, stirring often to prevent lumps from forming.

Step 2.   Reduce heat and simmer, stirring often, for 15 to 20 minutes or until polenta pulls away from the sides of the pan. Add the butter, stirring until the texture of the polenta becomes smooth and creamy. (An alternative method would be to stir the simmering polenta for about 5 minutes and then set it in a bain-marie for up to 45 minutes.)

Step 3.   Pour into a lightly-buttered, 9 by 13-inch baking dish and set aside to cool and thicken.

Step 4.   To make marinade, cut the fennel bulb in half and then thinly slice. Place in a small bowl.

Step 5.   Finely mince the onion, lemon peel, rosemary, parsley and thyme and add to the bowl. Add the vinegar and olive oil, stirring to combine.

Step 6.   Place the chicken breasts in a shallow baking pan and pour over the marinade, turning the chicken to coat all sides. Cover and marinate for 2 hours. (If the chicken is not fully submerged in the marinade, turn the breasts over again after 1 hour.)

Step 7.   To prepare vegetables, cut the fennel bulbs in half vertically and the tomatoes in half horizontally. Cut off the ends of the asparagus and peel the stems. Set aside.

Step 8. Cut the cooked artichokes in half and remove all of the tough outer leaves.

Step 9. Preheat the grill, according to manufacturer's directions, and lightly season with oil. The temperature of the grill should be moderately hot.

Step 10. Brush the cut sides of the fennel and tomato halves with a little olive oil.

Step 11. Cut the polenta into 4-inch squares. Then cut each square in half diagonally, to make triangles. Brush one side of the polenta with a little olive oil.

Step 12. To grill, place the fennel pieces, cut-side-down, on the outer edges of the grill (medium heat) and grill for 15 to 20 minutes, turning as needed, to brown on all sides.

Step 13. Meanwhile, remove chicken from marinade (reserve marinade) and place on the grill over moderate heat. Grill, turning once and brushing with reserved marinade, for 8 to 10 minutes or until chicken meat feels firm to the touch.

Step 14. When you turn over the chicken, place the polenta and the tomato halves, cut-sides-down, on the grill over a medium heat. Grill, turning once and brushing with additional oil as needed, for 2 to 4 minutes per side or until heated through. Season vegetables with salt and pepper to taste.

Step 15. Remove vegetables from grill and arrange at one end of a warm serving platter. Arrange chicken in the center and grilled polenta at the other end. Garnish with sprigs of fresh thyme, if desired.

Yield: 4 servings (Pictured on page 107.)

GRILLED CHICKEN BREAST
WITH WILD MUSHROOM MARSALA SAUCE

Relish

2	medium tomatoes
3	cloves garlic, peeled
1	small jalapeño pepper, seeded
8	to 10 fresh basil leaves
2	tablespoons balsamic vinegar

Vegetables

16	to 20 snow peas
2	medium red onions, peeled
2	small red bell peppers
2	or 3 zucchini
2	or 3 yellow squash
1	tablespoon canola oil

Marinade

2	to 3 tablespoons fresh lemon juice
2	to 3 tablespoons dark soy sauce
2	tablespoons chopped fresh basil leaves

Sauce

2	cloves garlic, peeled
½	pound wild mushrooms (such as Shiitake, Chantrelles, porcini, or oyster mushrooms)
1	tablespoon canola oil
1	cup Marsala wine
½	cup Brown Sauce/ Sauce Espagñole (page 38)
8	to 10 fresh basil leaves
2	ounces cold unsalted butter
2	chicken breasts, halved, with wing bone left on and skin removed
2	tablespoons canola oil

Step 1.   To prepare relish, score an "X" on the bottom of each tomato. Place in boiling water for 15 to 20 seconds. Remove and plunge into ice water to loosen their skins. Cool slightly and then peel, remove the seeds and cut in small (¼-inch) dice to make a *concassée*.

Step 2.   Mince the garlic. Cut off the ends of the jalapeño pepper, remove seeds and cut half of the pepper into very small (⅛-inch) dice, to make about ½ teaspoon. (If you prefer a spicy relish, mince the remaining half of the jalapeño as well.)

Step 3.   Stack the basil leaves on top of each other and roll up (like a cigar). Cut into very thin strips (called a *chiffonade*) and place in a bowl along with the garlic, jalapeño pepper and the tomato concassée. Stir in the vinegar until combined. Cover and refrigerate until ready to serve.

Step 4.   To prepare vegetables, snap off the stems and pull any strings from the snow peas; cut into julienne strips. Cut the red onions into julienne strips.

Step 5.   Cut off the top and bottom of the red pepper. Cut in half and remove the seeds. Flatten each half and remove the membrane. Cut into julienne strips.

Step 6.   Cut the zucchini and yellow squash into 2 to 3-inch-long pieces. Cut into quarters and then trim each into a football-shaped piece (sometimes called a *tourner*). Set aside.

Step 7.   To prepare marinade, combine the lemon juice, soy sauce and basil in a small bowl. Arrange chicken in a shallow baking dish. Pour the marinade over the chicken, turning to coat all sides evenly. Marinate for about 15 minutes.

Step 8.   Meanwhile, to prepare sauce, mince the garlic and trim off the stems from the mushrooms. Stack the basil leaves and cut into a chiffonade as described above. Heat the canola oil in a heavy sauté pan over moderate heat. When oil is hot, add the garlic and sauté for about 1 minute. Add the mushrooms and sauté for 2 to 3 minutes longer or until tender.

Step 9.   *Take pan off the flame.* Pour in the Marsala, return pan to moderate heat and deglaze, loosening the cooked particles on the bottom. Cook for 1 to 2 minutes longer or until reduced to one-half. Add the Brown Sauce/Sauce Espagñole and bring to a rapid boil.

Step 10. Add all but 1 tablespoon of the basil chiffonade and 1 tablespoon of the butter, whisking constantly. Add remaining butter, a tablespoon at a time, whisking to incorporate. Remove from heat and keep warm.

Step 11. To assemble, heat the 2 tablespoons canola oil in a heavy sauté pan over moderate heat. Remove chicken from marinade, shaking off the excess. When oil is hot, add the chicken and sauté for 4 to 5 minutes per side, turning once, or until golden brown. Remove and keep warm in oven.

Step 12. Return pan to moderate heat and add the remaining tablespoon of canola oil. When oil is hot, add the zucchini and squash. Sauté for 2 to 3 minutes. Remove and keep warm. Add red onions and sauté for 1 to 2 minutes. Add the snow peas and sauté for about 1 minute longer or until peas are tender but still crispy.

Step 13. Arrange some sautéed vegetables on each plate and top with a sautéed chicken breast. Arrange the yellow squash and zucchini around the outside of the chicken.

Step 14. Pour sauce over one corner of the chicken breast and onto some of the vegetables. Finally, place 1 teaspoon of relish on opposite sides of the plate and garnish with remaining basil chiffonade, if desired.

Yield: 4 servings

CHICKEN MADRAS
WITH CHICKPEA PUREE & MANGO MAYONNAISE

Mayonnaise

1   cup Basic Mayonnaise (page 43) or purchased mayonnaise
1   large ripe mango
2   tablespoons honey
1   teaspoon fresh mint

Purée

2   cups cooked chickpeas (garbanzo beans)
3   garlic cloves, peeled
1   to 2 tablespoons fresh lemon juice
3   tablespoons olive oil
1   tablespoon sesame oil (or sesame paste or *Tahini*)

Chicken

1   large clove garlic, peeled
½   small onion, peeled
1   small piece fresh ginger (about 2 tsp.)
4   boneless chicken thighs, with skin removed
¼   cup all-purpose flour
4   tablespoons peanut oil
2   tablespoons Madras curry powder
⅛   ground white pepper
1¼ cups Basic Chicken Stock (page 31)
¾   cup half-and-half
2   tablespoons mango chutney

1   teaspoon fresh cilantro
3   cups cooked Basmati rice (optional)

Step 1.   Prepare the mayonnaise as directed. Peel the mango, cut into pieces and place in a bowl. Chop the mint. Using a hand blender, process the mango until puréed. Stir in the mayonnaise, honey and chopped mint until well blended. Cover and chill for 30 minutes.

Step 2.   To prepare the purée, place garbanzo beans and the garlic in the bowl of a food processor fitted with a metal blade. Process for 1 to 2 minutes or until smooth. Add the lemon juice, olive oil and sesame oil and process until emulsified. Season to taste with salt and white pepper. Set aside.

Step 3.   Finely chop the garlic, onion and ginger. Heat the oil in a heavy sauté pan over moderate heat. Dust the chicken with flour, shaking off the excess.

Step 4.   When oil is hot, add the chicken and sauté for 3 to 4 minutes per side, turning once, or until chicken has browned evenly. Remove the chicken from pan and keep warm in the oven.

Step 5.   Return pan to moderate heat. When pan is hot, add the onion and sauté for 1 to 2 minutes or until translucent. Add the garlic, ginger, curry powder and white pepper and continue to sauté for 1 to 2 minutes longer.

Step 6.   Pour in the chicken stock and deglaze, loosening the cooked particles on the bottom of the pan. Cook for 1 to 2 minutes longer. Add the half-and-half and the chutney, stirring to combine. Reduce heat and simmer for 7 to 8 minutes or until sauce thickens slightly.

Step 7.   Return chicken to pan and simmer until heated thoroughly. Adjust seasoning with salt and white pepper, as needed.

Step 8.   To serve, arrange a piece of chicken on each plate. Spoon (or pipe using a pastry bag) some chickpea purée on both sides of the plate. Garnish with a dollop of mango mayonnaise and a sprinkling of chopped cilantro. Serve Basmati rice as an accompaniment, if desired.

Yield: 4 servings

CHICKEN PAPRIKASH
WITH APPLE CHUTNEY

Chutney
½ cup golden raisins
    Warm water
1 large Granny Smith apple
1 Anjou pear
½ bunch fresh mint
1 small serrano or jalapeño pepper
1 to 2 tablespoons fresh lemon juice
1 tablespoon fruit-flavored honey

2 medium tomatoes
3 shallots, peeled

4 cloves garlic, peeled
1 cup Seasoned Flour (page 120)
1 chicken (about 2½ lbs.), cut into 6 pieces
¼ cup olive oil
¼ cup sweet Hungarian or regular paprika
1 cup dry white wine
1 cup Basic Chicken Stock (page 31)
½ cup sour cream
2 tablespoons fresh lemon juice

Thin potato pancakes (optional)

Step 1. To prepare chutney, soften (or *plump*) the raisins in enough warm water to cover for 10 to 15 minutes. Core and chop the apple into small (¼-inch) dice. Core and chop the pear into small (¼-inch) dice. Finely chop the mint.

Step 2. Cut off the end of the jalapeño pepper, remove seeds and cut half of the pepper into very small (⅛-inch) dice, to make about ½ teaspoon. (If you prefer a spicy chutney, mince the remaining half of the jalapeño as well.)

Step 3. Drain the raisins well and place in a small bowl. Add the apples, pears, pepper, mint, lemon juice and honey, mixing well to combine. Season to taste with salt. Cover and refrigerate until ready to use.

Step 4. Score an "X" on the bottom of each tomato and place in a pan of boiling water to blanch for 15 to 20 seconds. Remove tomatoes with a slotted spoon and plunge them into a bowl of ice water to stop the cooking process. Peel, cut in half and squeeze out the seeds. Cut into small (¼-inch) dice. Chop the shallots and mince the garlic; set aside.

Step 5. Preheat the oven to 350°F.

Step 6. Prepare the Seasoned Flour as directed and measure out about ½ cup. Place in a shallow pan. Dredge the chicken pieces in the seasoned flour, turning to coat all sides, and shake off any excess.

Step 7. Heat the oil in a heavy, 6-quart pan over moderate heat. When oil is hot, add the chicken and sauté for 2 to 3 minutes or until golden brown on all sides. Add the shallots and cloves of garlic and sauté for 1 to 2 minutes longer.

Step 8. Add the paprika and continue to cook until slightly browned. Stir in the tomatoes, wine and chicken broth. Bring to a simmer.

Step 9 Cover and place in the preheated oven to braise for 45 to 50 minutes or until chicken is cooked. Pierce the chicken with a fork to test doneness. When the juices run clear the chicken is done. Remove from oven and transfer chicken to a serving platter; keep warm in the oven.

Step 10. Blend the sour cream and lemon juice into the pan drippings. Pour through a fine strainer or cheesecloth into a serving bowl. Offer apple chutney as an accompaniment and potato pancakes, if desired.

Yield: 4 servings

BUTTERMILK PAN-FRIED CHICKEN

1   **chicken (about 2½ lbs.), cut into 8 pieces**
1   **cup buttermilk**

Seasoned Flour
1   **to 2 teaspoons granulated (dried) garlic**
2   **teaspoons cayenne pepper**
1   **teaspoon onion powder**

1   **teaspoon baking powder**
1   **cup all-purpose flour**
½   **teaspoon salt**
1   **teaspoon ground black pepper**

2   **cups solid vegetable shortening**

Step 1.   Place the chicken in a shallow pan and cover with the buttermilk, turning to coat all sides of the chicken.

Step 2.   Cover and refrigerate for at least 8 to 10 hours or overnight.

Step 3.   To prepare seasoned flour, combine the garlic, cayenne pepper, onion powder, baking powder, flour, salt and black pepper in a small bowl. Mix until well blended.

Step 4.   Heat the vegetable shortening in a deep-sided, heavy pan over medium heat to a temperature of 325° to 340°F.

Step 5.   Remove chicken from the buttermilk, shaking off the excess milk. Reserve the buttermilk. Roll the chicken in seasoned flour and dip a second time into the buttermilk. Shake off any excess buttermilk and roll the pieces again in the seasoned flour. Set aside.

Step 6   When oil is hot, carefully lower the chicken pieces into the hot oil with a pair of long tongs. The oil should cover no more than one half of the chicken. Take care that the oil does not become too hot.

Step 7.   Cover the pan and fry for 8 to 10 minutes. Lift off cover, turn the chicken over using the tongs and continue to fry, uncovered, for 25 minutes longer or until cooked. Pierce the chicken with a fork to test doneness. When the juices run clear the chicken is done.

Step 8.   Remove the chicken from the oil and drain on a paper towel before serving.

Yield: 4 to 6 servings

BRAISED CHICKEN PORTUGUESE

3   medium tomatoes
1   onion, peeled
6   cloves garlic, peeled
10 to 12 large mushrooms, trimmed

Seasoned Flour
½   cup all-purpose flour
1   clove granulated (dried) garlic
½   tablespoon onion powder
1   teaspoon salt
2   teaspoons ground black pepper

⅛   teaspoon dried thyme
⅛   teaspoon crushed dried rosemary

1   chicken (about 2½ lbs.), cut into 6 pieces
¼   cup olive oil
¾   cup dry white wine
1   cup Basic Chicken Stock (page 31)
¼   cup parsley

Loaf of sourdough bread
Additional chopped parsley

Step 1. Score an "X" on the bottom of each tomato and place in a large pan of boiling water to blanch for 15 seconds. Remove tomatoes with a slotted spoon and plunge them into a bowl of ice water to stop the cooking process. Peel, cut in half and squeeze out the seeds. Cut into small (¼-inch) dice. Chop the onion and the garlic. Cut the mushrooms into thin slices.

Step 2. To prepare seasoned flour combine with the flour, garlic, onion powder, salt, black pepper, thyme and rosemary, mixing until well blended. Dredge the chicken pieces in the seasoned flour, turning to coat all sides, and shake off any excess.

Step 3. Heat the oil in a heavy, 6-quart pan over moderate heat. When oil is hot, add the chicken pieces and cook for 3 to 4 minutes or until golden brown on all sides.

Step 4. Remove chicken and keep warm in a 350°F oven, and return pan to heat. When pan is hot, add onion, mushrooms, tomatoes and garlic. Continue to cook for 3 to 4 minutes longer.

Step 5. *Take pan off the flame.* Pour in the wine, return pan to moderate heat and deglaze, loosening the cooked particles on the bottom. Cook for 1 to 2 minutes longer. Stir in the stock and parsley; return chicken to the pan. Cover and return to hot oven to braise for 45 to 50 minutes or until chicken is cooked. Pierce the chicken with a fork to test doneness. When the juices run clear the chicken is done.

Step 6. For a special presentation, cut off the top third of a round loaf of sourdough bread. Scoop out the insides (and reserve for other uses). Fill the hollowed-out loaf with the chicken and top with some of the sauce. Garnish with additional chopped parsley. Offer remaining sauce as an accompaniment.

Yield: 4 to 6 servings

SONOMA KIEV
WITH STEAMED BABY VEGETABLES

Compound Butter

¼ cup marinated sun-dried tomatoes, drained

2 tablespoons chives

½ pound butter, room temperature

¼ cup fresh lemon juice

½ cup Seasoned Flour (page 120)

2 boneless chicken breasts, halved and skin removed

4 eggs

¾ to 1 cup vegetable oil

2 cups soft fresh breadcrumbs

Vegetables

¼ pound snap peas, trimmed

¼ pound baby yellow squash

¼ pound baby carrots, peeled

3 or 4 small Japanese eggplants

Step 1. To prepare butter, cut the sun-dried tomatoes into very small (⅛-inch) dice (called a *brunoise*) and mince the chives. Place both in a bowl and add the softened butter and the lemon juice, whisking to combine. Continue to whip vigorously for 2 to 3 minutes or until well incorporated.

Step 2. Place the mixture on a sheet of parchment paper and roll into 1-inch-thick cylinder. Refrigerate for at least one hour or until butter is firmly set.

Step 3. Prepare Seasoned Flour as directed on page 120. Measure out ½ cup and place in a shallow pan. Set aside.

Step 4. Lay the chicken breast flat on the work surface in between two sheets of plastic wrap and pound to a thickness of ¼-inch. Discard the top layer of plastic.

Step 5. Place 2 tablespoons of butter mixture in the center of each breast. Fold and re-shape the breast, tucking the ends of the roll under to completely enclose the butter. Chill for 2 hours.

Step 6. Crack eggs into a shallow bowl and lightly beat. Remove chicken from refrigerator and roll in the seasoned flour, shaking off any excess, and then dip into the beaten eggs.

Step 7. Roll chicken in the flour a second time and then back into the beaten eggs.

Step 8. Finally, roll each breast in the breadcrumbs, taking care to completely cover the chicken with crumbs. Chill in the refrigerator for about one hour.

Step 9.   Preheat the oven to 350°F.

Step 10. Heat the oil in a deep-sided, heavy pan over medium heat to a temperature of 375°F. Carefully lower the chicken into the hot oil with tongs and fry, turning occasionally, for 4 to 6 minutes or until golden brown. Remove with a slotted spoon and drain on paper towels.

Step 11. Transfer to a baking pan and place in the preheated oven and bake for 10 minutes.

Step 12. Meanwhile, place the carrots and eggplant in a steaming rack over boiling water. Cover and steam for 2 to 3 minutes. Add the squash and the snap peas and steam for 1 to 2 minutes longer or until the vegetables are tender but still crisp. Transfer to a warm serving platter. Remove chicken from oven and arrange over the vegetables.

Yield: 4 servings

CHICKEN DIJON
WITH MUSHROOM PILAF

1   large shallot, peeled
2   small cloves garlic, peeled
1   red onion, peeled
1   red bell pepper
12 asparagus
1   Belgium endive, trimmed
2   tablespoons fresh lemon juice
¼   cup water
4   tablespoons vegetable oil
2   boneless chicken breasts, halved
    and skin removed

Sauce
2   tablespoons coarse Dijon-style mustard
1   tablespoon regular Dijon-style mustard
¼   cup dry white wine
1   cup half-and-half

1   teaspoon minced chives
    Mushroom pilaf (optional)

Step 1.   Mince the shallot and the garlic. Cut the red onion into thin julienne strips. Cut off the top and bottom of the red pepper. Cut in half and remove the seeds. Flatten each half and remove the membrane. Cut into thin julienne strips. Cut off the bottoms of the asparagus and peel the stems using a vegetable peeler. Set aside.

Step 2.   Trim off the bottom of the Belgian endive and split in half lengthwise. Cut into a *chiffonade* and place in a small bowl. Add the lemon juice and water, mixing to combine.

Step 3.   Heat 2 tablespoons of the oil in a heavy sauté pan over moderate heat. When the oil is hot, add the chicken and sauté for 2 to 3 minutes per side, turning once, or until chicken is brown on both sides and slightly firm to the touch. Remove and keep warm in the oven. Return pan to moderate heat and add another tablespoon of oil. When the oil is hot, add the shallots and sauté for 1 to 2 minutes. Add the garlic and sauté for 1 to 2 minutes longer.

Step 4.   *Take pan off the flame.* Pour in the wine, return pan to moderate heat and deglaze, loosening the cooked particles on the bottom. Cook for 4 to 5 minutes longer or until reduced by two-thirds. Stir in the Dijon mustards until blended. Then add the half-and-half, reduce heat and simmer over low heat. Return chicken to the pan and keep warm.

Step 5.   Meanwhile, heat remaining tablespoon of oil in another heavy sauté pan over moderate heat. When oil is hot, add the onion and sauté for about 1 minute or until translucent. Add the red pepper and asparagus and sauté for 2 to 3 minutes or until tender but still crisp. Add Belgium endive and sauté for 1 minute longer.

Step 6.   To serve, place a spoonful of sautéed vegetables on each plate and arrange a breast of chicken on top. Spoon a little sauce over the corner of each breast and garnish with a sprinkling of minced chives. Serve with mushroom pilaf, if desired.

Yield: 4 servings

GRILLED FLANK STEAK AMERICAINE

Marinade
1   small clove garlic, peeled
¼   cup Worchestershire sauce
3   tablespoons red wine vinegar
1   teaspoon onion powder
1   teaspoon celery salt
½   teaspoon salt
1   teaspoon ground black pepper
⅔   cup olive oil

1   flank steak (about 1½ lbs.), trimmed

Vegetables
2   zucchini
8   to 10 large mushrooms
8   to 10 cherry tomatoes
8   mini red potatoes, parboiled

¼   cup Basil Butter(page 102)

Step 1.   To prepare marinade, mince the garlic and place in a large, shallow baking pan. Add the Worchestershire, vinegar, onion powder, celery salt, salt, black pepper and olive oil, stirring until combined.

Step 2.   Place the flank steak in the marinade. (Be sure that the meat is lying flat in the marinade.) Cover and refrigerate for about 4 hours, turning the meat over after two hours.

Step 3.   To prepare the vegetables, cut the zucchini into 2-inch pieces. Thread the mushrooms, cherry tomatoes, red potatoes and zucchini on flat metal skewers.

Step 4.   Remove flank steak from the refrigerator and allow to stand at room temperature for about 15 minutes.

Step 5.   Meanwhile, preheat the grill, according to manufacturer's directions, and lightly season with vegetable oil. The temperature of the grill should be moderately hot.

Step 6.   Remove the flank steak from the marinade (reserve marinade), shake off the excess liquid and place on the grill over medium heat. Grill over a medium-high heat for 10 to 12 minutes, turning once and basting with reserved marinade as needed.

Step 7.   To test for desired doneness, press the surface of the meat with your finger. If you can press your finger into the meat with little or no resistance, it is rare to medium rare. If the meat resists the pressure of your finger and feels "spring-like", it is medium to well done.

Step 8.   When you turn the flank steak over, arrange the skewered vegetables over medium heat and grill, turning occasionally, for 2 to 3 minutes, basting with the garlic-flavored oil.

Step 9.   Remove the flank steak from the grill and transfer to a cutting board. Cut meat into slanting, ⅛-inch-thick slices and serve the vegetable skewers as an accompaniment.

Yield: 4 servings

POACHED BEEF TENDERLOIN
WITH SABAYON & WILD MUSHROOM SAUTE

Poaching Liquid

2 quarts Basic Beef Stock (page 33)
2 carrots, peeled
2 stalks celery
1 small onion, peeled
1 bunch parsley
1 bunch fresh tarragon

1 piece of beef tenderloin
  (1½ to 2 lbs.), trimmed

Sabayon Sauce

6 egg yolks
2 teaspoons Worchestershire sauce
1 cup reserved Basic Beef Stock
2 teaspoons reserved tarragon leaves
1 tablespoon tarragon vinegar

1 pound mushrooms
½ to 1 pound wild mushrooms (such as
  Chantrelles or morels)
4 tablespoons unsalted butter

Step 1. To make poaching liquid, cut the carrots into thin slices. Cut the celery into small pieces and thinly slice the onion. Set aside.

Step 2. Pull the leaves off of the parsley, reserving them for other uses, and set the stems aside. Pull the leaves off the tarragon, mince them finely and reserve for making the sauce. Set the stems aside.

Step 3. Twist or cut off the stems from the mushrooms. The mushroom caps will be sautéed later. Place the stems in a heavy, 6-quart stockpot.

Step 4. Pour in the stock and add the carrots, celery and onions. Twist the parsley stems to extract more flavor and drop into the stockpot. Add the tarragon stems. Place stockpot over low heat until poaching liquid comes to a full simmer.

Step 5. Carefully, lower the beef tenderloin into the stock and poach, uncovered, for 14 to 18 minutes or until internal temperature of the meat reaches 130°F (medium rare).

Step 6. Remove from stock (reserving 1 cup for making the sauce) and place in an oven to keep warm.

Step 7. To make sabayon, place the 1 cup reserved stock in a small pan and bring to simmer over low heat.

Step 8.   Position a wide mixing bowl over a small pan of water, taking care to see that the bottom of the bowl does not touch the water in the pan. (You will be making the sauce in the mixing bowl and it is important to control the heat.)

Step 9.   Place yolks in the mixing bowl. Whisk in the Worchestershire, reserved minced tarragon and the vinegar.

Step 10.   Slowly, whisk in the hot stock until the sauce becomes frothy and begins to thicken to a sauce-like consistency.

Step 11.   Transfer to a double boiler and keep warm (about 110° to 120°F).

Step 12.   To make mushrooms, cut the mushroom caps into thin slices. Melt the butter in heavy, 10-inch sauté pan over medium heat. When butter is hot, add the sliced mushrooms and sauté quickly, shaking the pan often, for 2 to 3 minutes or until mushrooms are tender.

Step 13.   To serve, slice the beef on a bias into 8 to 10 slices and arrange on a warm serving platter accompanied by the sautéed mushroom caps. Spoon some of the sabayon sauce over the beef and garnish with additional fresh tarragon. Offer remaining sabayon alongside.

Yield: 6 to 8 servings (Pictured on page 108.)

ANCHO CHILE BEEF
WITH BLACK BEAN & CORN CONFETTI

Tomato-Cilantro Relish

2 ripe tomatoes
½ bunch fresh cilantro
2 tablespoons fresh lime juice
1 small jalapeño pepper (optional)

Confetti

1 clove chopped garlic
1 tablespoon olive oil
½ cup cooked corn kernels
¼ cup cooked black beans
½ teaspoon ground cumin

3 tablespoons corn oil
8 beef medallions (3 oz. each)

Sauce

6 cloves garlic, peeled
1 small onion, peeled
2 medium tomatoes
1 tablespoon ground ancho chile powder
¼ cup red wine vinegar
1¼ cups Basic Beef Stock (page 33)
3 tablespoons fresh oregano, stems removed
2 tablespoons fresh lime juice

8 soft corn tortillas

Step 1. To make relish, chop the tomatoes into small (¼-inch) dice and place in a small bowl. Cut off the end of the jalapeño pepper, remove seeds and cut half of the pepper into very small (⅛-inch) dice, to make about ½ teaspoon. (If you prefer a spicy relish, mince the remaining half of the jalapeño as well.)

Step 2. Chop the cilantro and add to the tomatoes. Stir in the lime juice and jalapeño pepper. Cover and chill until ready to use.

Step 3. To make confetti, mince the garlic. Heat the olive oil in a heavy sauté pan over moderate heat. When oil is hot, add the corn and black beans and sauté for 1 to 2 minutes.

Step 4. Add garlic and cumin seed. Set aside and keep warm.

Step 5. To blanch tomatoes, score an "X" on the bottom of each tomato and place in a large pan of boiling water to blanch for 15 seconds. Remove tomatoes with a slotted spoon and plunge them into a bowl of ice water. Peel tomatoes, cut in half and squeeze out the seeds. Cut into medium (½-inch) dice. Mince the garlic and coarsely chop the oregano. Set both aside.

Step 6. Heat corn oil in heavy sauté pan over moderate heat. When oil is hot, add the medallions and sauté for 3 to 4 minutes, turning once, or until browned on both sides. Remove and keep warm in the oven.

Step 7. To make sauce, return pan to heat. When pan is hot, add the onion and sauté lightly for 2 to 3 minutes or until translucent. Add the garlic, tomatoes, and chile powder; sauté for 1 to 2 minutes.

Step 8. Add wine vinegar and deglaze, loosening the cooked particles on the bottom of the pan. Cook for 2 to 3 minutes longer or until reduced slightly.

Step 9. Add beef broth, oregano and lime juice and continue to reduce for 2 minutes longer. Return the medallions to the sauce to heat thoroughly.

Step 10. To serve, place two medallions on a warm plate and spoon sauce over the top.

Step 11. Spoon some relish on each side of the plate, garnish with the corn and black bean confetti and serve warm tortillas as an accompaniment.

Yield: 4 to 6 servings

SAUTEED BEEF
WITH LEMON GRASS

¾ to 1 pound beef sirloin
(or flank steak), trimmed

Marinade
2 tablespoons light soy sauce
1 tablespoon dry sherry
2 teaspoons cornstarch
2 teaspoons vegetable oil

2 tablespoons vegetable oil
4 cloves garlic, peeled

2 stalks of lemon grass
½ red bell pepper
4 scallions
1 tablespoon fish sauce
1 tablespoon dark soy sauce
1 teaspoon sesame oil
1 teaspoon granulated sugar

Deep-fried rice noodles
Fresh cilantro leaves
(or purple opal basil leaves)

Step 1. To make marinade, thinly slice the beef across the grain and place in a bowl. Add the soy sauce, sherry, cornstarch and oil, stirring after each addition to coat the meat evenly. Cover and marinate for 15 to 30 minutes.

Step 2. Meanwhile, mince the garlic. Using only the hearts, cut the lemon grass stalks into thin slices. Cut off the top and bottom of the bell pepper. Cut in half and remove the seeds. Flatten each half and remove the membrane. Cut into julienne strips.

Step 3. Cut the scallions on a bias into ½-inch-long pieces. Reserve most of the greens for garnish.

Step 4. Heat the vegetable oil in a heavy, 10-inch sauté pan. When oil is hot, add the beef strips and sauté for 1 to 2 minutes or until slightly pink. Remove and keep warm.

Step 5. Add the garlic and sauté for 5 to 10 seconds or until garlic turns fragrant and begins to flavor the oil. Take care not to burn the garlic.

Step 6. Add the lemon grass and sauté lightly for 1 to 2 minutes or until tender but still crisp. Add the red pepper and green onion and sauté for 1 to 2 minutes longer.

Step 7. Stir in the fish sauce and soy sauce, deglazing to loosen the cooked particles on the bottom of the pan. Cook for 1 to 2 minutes longer to reduce slightly.

Step 8. Return the beef to the sauce until heated thoroughly. Stir in the sugar and sesame oil.

Step 9. Serve over deep-fried rice noodles and garnish with cilantro leaves.

Yield: 4 servings

GRILLED TERIYAKI BEEF KEBABS

1¼ pounds beef sirloin

Marinade
1 medium-size piece of ginger, peeled
6 cloves garlic, peeled
6 scallions
2 tablespoons sesame oil

1 cup dark soy sauce
½ cup dry sherry
½ cup brown sugar

Vegetable oil
4 or 6 metal skewers,
(6 to 8 inches long)

Step 1. Trim the beef of any excess fat and cut into 1-inch cubes.

Step 2. To make marinade, mince the ginger and the garlic. Chop the scallions into small pieces. Place the ginger, garlic and scallions into a bowl. Add the sesame oil, soy sauce, sherry and brown sugar, stirring to combine.

Step 3. Place the beef into the marinade, taking care that the marinade completely covers the pieces. Cover and refrigerate for at least 12 hours or overnight.

Step 4. Preheat the grill, according to manufacturer's directions, and lightly season with vegetable oil. The temperature of the grill should be medium-high.

Step 5. Remove the steak from the marinade (reserve marinade). Shake off any excess marinade and then thread the meat onto metal skewers.

Step 6. Place on the preheated grill over medium-high heat and grill for 6 to 8 minutes, turning once and basting with reserved marinade as needed, or until meat is medium rare and evenly cooked on all sides.

Step 7. To test for desired doneness, press the surface of the meat with your finger. If you can press your finger into the meat with little or no resistance, it is rare to medium rare. If the meat resists the pressure of your finger and feels "spring-like", it is medium to well done.

Step 8. Transfer to a warm platter to serve.

Yield: 4 to 6 servings

PORK TENDERLOIN
WITH RHUBARB SAUCE & SWEET POTATO HAY

Sauce

½ cup fresh rhubarb, trimmed
1 large Granny Smith apple
1 very small piece ginger, peeled
2 tablespoons fresh lemon juice
2 tablespoons sesame oil
1 tablespoon honey
2 cups Brown Sauce/Sauce Espagñole (page 38)

Relish

2 large Granny Smith apples
¼ bunch fresh mint, stems removed
1 teaspoon lemon juice
1 to 2 teaspoons honey

Sweet Potato Hay

1 or 2 large sweet potatoes, peeled
1 cup vegetable oil

Pork

4 pieces pork tenderloin (6 oz. each)
4 tablespoons coarsely-cracked black pepper
2 tablespoons sesame oil

Vegetables

2 or 3 stalks bok choy, trimmed
2 large carrots, peeled
2 large zucchini, trimmed
¼ pound snow peas, trimmed
1 tablespoon sesame oil

Step 1. To prepare the sauce, finely chop the rhubarb, apple and ginger. Place the rhubarb and apple in a bowl and add lemon juice, tossing to combine.

Step 2. Heat the sesame oil in a heavy sauté pan over medium heat. When oil is very hot, add the ginger and sweat for 2 to 3 minutes or until tender. Add the apple and the rhubarb and cook for about 1 minute.

Step 3. Stir in the lemon juice and honey and cook for 3 to 4 minutes or until the apples are soft. Add the Sauce Espagñole and simmer, uncovered, for 20 to 30 minutes or until reduced by one-half.

Step 4. Remove from heat, cool slightly and the purée with a hand blender or in a food processor. Pour through a fine strainer or cheesecloth. (The sauce may be prepared 2 to 3 days in advance and kept covered in the refrigerator, if desired.)

Step 5. To prepare relish, coarsely chop the apples and toss with the lemon juice to prevent discoloration. Stack the mint leaves, one on top of the other, and roll up (like a cigar). Cut into thin strips (called a *chiffonade*) and add to the apples. Stir in the honey until combined. Refrigerate.

Step 6.   To prepare the hay, peel the sweet potatoes. Using a mandoline, thinly slice the potatoes so they look like *very thin* strings (do not rinse).

Step 7.   Heat the 1 cup of oil in a heavy sauté pan over moderate heat to a temperature of 325°F.

Step 8.   Sprinkle some of the sweet potato "strings" into the oil. (Do not crowd.) The strings should cook separately. Fry for 2 to 3 minutes or until slightly brown and then remove with a slotted spoon and drain on paper towels. Repeat process.

Step 9.   To prepare pork, preheat the oven to 350°F. Trim off and discard any fat from the pork and then roll each piece in the cracked pepper.

Step 10.   Heat the 2 tablespoons sesame oil in a heavy, 10-inch sauté pan over moderate heat. When the oil is hot, add the pork and sauté for 8 to 10 minutes, turning once, or until seared on both sides. Transfer to the preheated oven and cook for 8 to 10 minutes longer or until internal temperature of the pork reaches 150°F.

Step 11.   Meanwhile, to prepare the vegetables, cut the bok choy on a bias into 1-inch pieces. Cut the carrots and zucchini into 1-inch pieces. (See *tourner*, page 28 for a more decorative cut.) Snap off the stems from the snow peas.

Step 12.   Heat the remaining tablespoon sesame oil in a heavy sauté pan over moderate heat. When oil is hot, add the carrots and sauté for 2 minutes. Add the bok choy and snow peas and sauté for 1 minute. Add the zucchini and sauté for 1 minute longer or until heated through.

Step 13.   To assemble, place sautéed vegetables on the center of a warm plate. Slice each pork loin into 3 or 4 pieces (called *medallions*) and arrange on the sides of the vegetables, overlapping slightly.

Step 14.   Spoon the hot sauce over the base of each pork medallion. Place a teaspoon of relish between each medallion and garnish the top of the vegetables with some sweet potato hay.

Yield: 8 servings (Pictured on page 106.)

SAUERBRATEN
WITH BRAISED RED CABBAGE

1 beef rump roast or bottom round
(3 to 4 lbs.)
Butcher's twine

Marinade
2 onions, peeled
1 carrot, peeled
1 stalk celery
4 cloves garlic, peeled
1 teaspoon salt
1 teaspoon ground black pepper
6 to 8 whole black peppercorns
2 bay leaves
¼ cup red wine vinegar
2 cups Basic Beef Stock (page 33)

2 tablespoons salad oil

Cabbage
1 head red cabbage (about 1½ lbs.)
1 small onion, peeled
2 large Granny Smith apples
2 to 3 tablespoons unsalted butter
½ cup red wine vinegar
¼ teaspoon salt
1 to 2 teaspoons granulated sugar
½ teaspoon celery or caraway seeds

Sauce
6 tablespoons unsalted butter
5 tablespoons all-purpose flour
1 tablespoon granulated sugar
2 cups reserved braising liquid
8 to 10 gingersnap cookies

Step 1.   To truss the beef, holding one end of a long piece of butcher's twine, slip it under the entire length of the roast. Bring up the end and loosely tie a knot. Loop the long end of the remaining twine over your wrist. Expand the loop large enough to fit over the roast. Slide the loop over the roast and secure, about an inch from the previous knot, by pulling the long end of the string hard enough to tighten the loop. Take care to keep each loop equally taut as you repeat the tying process, every inch or so, until entire roast has been laced. Secure with a knot.

Step 2.   To make marinade, cut the onions, carrot and celery into small (¼-inch) dice. Chop the garlic.

Step 3.   Combine onions, carrot, celery, garlic, salt, pepper, bay leaves, peppercorns, vinegar and stock in a large bowl. Add the trussed meat. Cover and refrigerate for 24 to 48 hours. The longer you marinate the beef, the more intense the flavor will be.

Step 4.   To braise, preheat oven to 350°F. Remove roast from marinade (reserving marinade) and pat dry.

Step 5.   Pour reserved marinade through a strainer. Keep both the liquid and the vegetables for separate use later on.

Step 6.   Heat the oil in a heavy, 6-quart braising pan over medium heat. When oil is hot, add the meat and sear until browned on all sides. Remove the meat and set aside.

Step 7.   Return pan to heat. When pan is hot, add the reserved vegetables and sauté for 2 to 3 minutes or until partially caramelized. Return meat to the pan. Pour in the reserved marinade. (If necessary, add additional beef stock to come half-way up the sides of the meat.)

Step 8.   Cover and place in the preheated oven. Braise for 2 to 2½ hours.

Step 9.   Meanwhile, to prepare cabbage, remove tough outer leaves from the cabbage. Remove core and cut the cabbage into thin slices. Rinse under cold water and drain. Cut the onion into small (¼-inch) dice. Peel and core the apple; cut into medium (½-inch) dice.

Step 10.   Melt the 2 tablespoons butter in a heavy, 6-quart saucepan over medium heat. When butter is hot, add the onions and sauté for 2 to 3 minutes. Add the cabbage, apples, vinegar, salt, sugar and celery seeds. Cover, reduce heat and braise for 35 to 45 minutes or until tender.

Step 11.   To prepare sauce, remove 2 cups braising liquid from the meat. Do this just fifteen minutes before the beef is done. Keep warm.

Step 12.   Melt the remaining 6 tablespoons butter in a heavy sauté pan over medium heat. When butter is hot, whisk in the flour (to a paste consistency) and cook, stirring constantly, for 2 to 3 minutes or until the roux bubbles and begins to color slightly. Add the sugar and cook until mixture begins to turn a dark, rich brown color.

Step 13.   Skim the braising liquid to remove any surface fat. Add the roux to the braising liquid, stirring to combine. Cover and finish cooking.

Step 14.   To serve, remove meat and set aside for about 5 minutes. Meanwhile, coarsely chop the gingersnaps in a mincer/chopper and stir into the braising liquid. Using a hand blender, blend sauce until smooth. Return pan to moderate heat and cook for 2 to 3 minutes or until slightly thickened.

Step 15.   Cut the meat, across the grain, into thin slices and arrange on a warm serving platter. Spoon some sauce over the top and offer the braised cabbage as an accompaniment.

Yield: About 8 servings

PORK ADOBO
WITH DRIED SHRIMP

2   pounds boneless pork shoulder

Marinade
8   cloves garlic, peeled
¾   cup red wine vinegar
2   tablespoons soy sauce
1   tablespoon fish sauce
3   or 4 bay leaves

2   tablespoons vegetable oil
1   medium onion
¾   cup Basic Chicken Stock (page 31)

Fried Shrimp
1   to 2 cups safflower oil
4   ounces dried shrimp

Steamed black sesame rice

Step 1. Trim any remaining fat from the pork and cut into 1½-inch cubes.

Step 2. To prepare marinade, mince the garlic and place in a bowl. Add the vinegar, soy sauce, fish sauce and bay leaves, stirring to combine. Add the pork, turning to coat all sides, cover and marinate in the refrigerator for 3 to 4 hours.

Step 3. Remove the pork from the marinade and drain, reserving the marinade liquid.

Step 4. Heat the oil in a heavy, 4-quart saucepan over moderate heat. When the oil is hot, add the pork and sauté until well browned.

Step 5. Meanwhile, slice the onions thinly. Add to the pan and sauté for 5 or 6 minutes or until translucent and soft. Add the reserved marinade and the stock. Reduce heat, cover and simmer for 18 to 20 minutes.

Step 6. Meanwhile, to prepare shrimp, heat 1 to 2 cups of oil in a heavy, deep-side pan over medium heat to a temperature of 350°F. Carefully, drop in the dried shrimp and fry for about 1 minute. Remove from oil, drain on paper towels and keep warm.

Step 7. To finish sauce, remove the pork and transfer to a warm oven. Skim off and discard any surface fat and place the pan over moderate heat. Cook for 5 to 8 minutes or until sauce has thickened and reduced to one-half. Return the pork to the sauce, stirring to combine.

Step 8. For a special presentation, lightly oil a round savarin (gelatin) mold, fill the ring with the steamed rice (seasoned with 2 tablespoons black sesame seeds) and pack firmly.

Step 9. Unmold the rice onto the center of a warm platter and ladle the pork adobo into the center of ring. Place the fried shrimp onto the top of the adobo and serve.

Yield: 6 to 8 servings

DESSERTS

CHAMPAGNE SORBET
WITH RASPBERRY COULIS IN TULIP COOKIE CUPS

Cookies

½ cup granulated sugar
4 egg whites
½ teaspoon vanilla extract
¾ cup all-purpose flour
1 tablespoon cornstarch
⅔ cup clarified butter

Coulis

2 pints fresh raspberries
¼ cup granulated sugar
⅓ cup fresh orange juice
1 tablespoon fresh lemon juice
1 tablespoon raspberry-flavored liqueur (Framboise)

Sorbet

1 cup plus 2 tablespoons (8 oz.) granulated sugar
1 to 1½ cups water
1¾ cups Brut sparkling wine
2 tablespoons fresh lemon juice

Fresh sprigs of mint
Extra fresh raspberries (optional)

Step 1. To prepare cookies, using a rubber spatula, combine the sugar, egg whites and vanilla in a bowl until just blended, taking care not to whip the mixture.

Step 2. Sift the flour with the cornstarch. Using a rubber spatula in a lifting motion, fold the flour into the egg whites until combined. Add the clarified butter, mixing to combine. Set aside and allow batter to rest for about 30 minutes.

Step 3. Preheat the oven 325°F. Place about 1 to 2 tablespoons of batter on a non-stick baking sheet *without sides* and using the back of the spoon, gently spread into a circle about 6 inches in diameter. Batter should be uniformly thin—enough to see through but not so thin that holes appear through the surface. Repeat with more batter, placing another circle (or two) about 2 inches apart on the baking sheet. (Note: If using a baking pan *with* sides, turn pan over and bake on the back side instead.)

Step 4. Place baking sheet in the preheated oven and bake for 5 to 8 minutes or until cookie begins to turn golden brown. Leaving the baking sheet in the oven, quickly remove cookies (one at a time) with a metal spatula and drape each cookie over an inverted wide-mouthed coffee cup or glass. You may need to press the cookie just slightly to conform to the shape of the cup, but if you do, be sure to leave a 3-inch-wide opening in the cookie for a scoop of sorbet. Repeat with remaining batter until all the cookie cups are baked.

Step 5.   To prepare coulis, combine raspberries, sugar, orange juice, lemon juice and liqueur in the bowl of a food processor fitted with a metal blade. Process until puréed.

Step 6.   Pour mixture through fine mesh strainer. Cover and refrigerate until ready to use or up to 3 days, if made in advance.

Step 7.   To prepare sorbet, combine sugar and ¾ cup of the water in a heavy, 2-quart saucepan over moderate heat. Bring to a boil, reduce heat and boil gently for 2 minutes or until mixture becomes a syrup. Remove from heat and allow to cool completely.

Step 8.   Stir in the sparkling wine, ¾ cup water and lemon juice.

Step 9.   Pour the mixture into the canister of an ice cream machine and freeze according to the manufacturer's directions.

Step 10.   To assemble, use an over-sized plate for presentation, allowing enough room for the sauce and its decoration. Place a heaping tablespoon (or so) of sauce in the center of each plate. Tilt the plate slightly, in each direction, to spread the sauce evenly. Use just enough sauce to thinly cover the plate; you should be able to see the bottom of the plate through the sauce.

Step 11.   Place one cookie inside a second one, creating a double layer or "flower blossom" effect. Fill the center of the cookie with a scoop of sorbet and place in the center of the sauce. Garnish with a few raspberries and a sprig of mint to serve.

Step 12.   For variations of this presentation, follow Step 10 on page 151. Or, try placing sauce only on one-half the plate and the filled cookie on the edge, leaving a bare space to contrast. Or, make a second sauce with a similar consistency and complimentary flavor, but contrasting color. Spoon some of each sauce on opposite sides of the plate. Then tilt the plate just until they meet in the middle but without mixing.

Yield: 6 to 8 servings (Pictured on page 144.)

STRAWBERRY SHERBET
IN CHILLED CHOCOLATE CUPS

Chocolate Cups

4   ounces white chocolate

4   ounces semi-sweet chocolate

8   paper muffin cups (3-oz. capacity)

2   cups fresh strawberries, hulled (or frozen strawberries without syrup)

1   cup granulated sugar

1   cup sour cream

½   teaspoon vanilla extract

½   cup heavy cream

1   tablespoon sour cream

Quartered strawberries

Step 1.   To make chocolate cups, coarsely chop the dark and white chocolate separately. Place the white chocolate in the top of a double boiler (or bain marie) and melt over low heat. Repeat procedure with the dark chocolate. Cool chocolates slightly until they are cool to the touch.

Step 2   Line a muffin pan with eight paper baking cups. To secure the paper cups in the pan, place a drop of chocolate in the bottom of each section, pressing the paper cup down until it adheres to the chocolate.

Step 3.   Using a pastry brush, paint one-half of the inside of each cup with white chocolate and the other half with semi-sweet chocolate. Place muffin pan in the refrigerator and chill until firm.

Step 4.   To make sherbet, place the 2 cups of strawberries in the bowl of a food processor fitted with a metal blade. Process with on/off bursts until chopped but not completely puréed. Transfer strawberries to a bowl and stir in the sugar. Cover and let stand to *macerate* for one hour.

Step 5.   After an hour, add the sour cream and vanilla, stirring to combine well. Transfer the mixture into the canister of an ice cream machine and freeze according to manufacturer's directions. Cover and store in the freezer until ready to serve.

Step 6.   Because you will be whipping cream and it is best to use very cold utensils when doing so, place a bowl and the beaters of your mixer in the freezer. Pour the cream and sour cream into the chilled bowl. Using the chilled utensils, whip the creams to medium-stiff peak consistency. Transfer cream to a pastry bag fitted with No. 4 star tip.

Step 7.   Remove chocolate cups from refrigerator and carefully peel the paper from each cup. Remember to handle the cups delicately, as chocolate melts at body temperature. Place a cup on a dessert plate and fill with a scoop of strawberry sherbet. Pipe a rosette of whipped cream on top and garnish each rosette with a piece of strawberry.

Yield: 4 servings

CHOCOLATE BREAD PUDDING WITH
BERRY SAUCE & ALMOND TUILES

TRUFFLED BANANA FRITTERS
WITH KIWI & TANGERINE COULIS

MENDOCINO POACHED PEAR ON CHOCOLATE WITH ALMOND-PEAR SAUCE

CHAMPAGNE SORBET WITH RASPBERRY
COULIS IN TULIP COOKIE CUPS

FRESH LEMON GRANITE

2 tablespoons lemon zest
2 cups fresh lemon juice
1 cup (non-carbonated) mineral water
¾ cup granulated sugar

2 tablespoons honey
3 or 4 whole lemons, cut in half lengthwise
    with flesh removed

Fresh sprigs of mint

Step 1. Finely mince the zest and place in a heavy, 2-quart saucepan. Add the lemon juice, mineral water, sugar and honey.

Step 2. Bring to a boil over medium heat, stirring to dissolve the sugar. Set aside to cool slightly. Transfer to a large bowl, cover and place in the freezer for 1 to 2 hours or until ice crystals have formed along the edges of the mixture.

Step 3. Using a hand blender, quickly break up the crystals until they are evenly distributed throughout the mixture. Return mixture to the freezer.

Step 4. Repeat process 3 to 4 more times, every 30 to 40 minutes, or until a crunchy yet slushy texture is reached.

Step 5. To serve, place 2 or 3 scoops of granité in each lemon half and garnish with a sprig of mint.

Yield: 6 to 8 servings

VARIATIONS

Pink Grapefruit Granité: Finely mince **2 tablespoons Ruby (pink) grapefruit zest** and place in a heavy, 2-quart saucepan. Add **2 cups fresh grapefruit juice**, 1 cup (non-carbonated) **mineral water**, **¾ cups granulated sugar** and **2 tablespoons honey**. Bring to a boil over medium heat, stirring to dissolve sugar. Set aside to cool. Transfer to a large bowl, cover and place in freezer for 1 to 2 hours or until ice crystals have formed along the edge of the mixture. Using a hand blender, quickly break up the ice crystals until they are evenly distributed throughout the mixture. Return to freezer. Repeat the process 3 to 4 more times, every 30 to 40 minutes, or until a crunchy yet slushy texture is reached.
Yield: 6 to 8 servings

Orange-Pomegranate Granité: Finely mince **2 tablespoons orange zest** and place in a heavy, 2-quart saucepan. Add **1½ cups fresh orange juice**, **½ cup pomegranate juice**, 1 cup (non-carbonated) **mineral water**, **¾ cups granulated sugar** and **2 tablespoons honey**. Bring to a boil over medium heat, stirring to dissolve sugar. Set aside to cool. Transfer to a large bowl, cover and place in freezer for 1 to 2 hours or until ice crystals have formed along the edges of the mixture. Using a hand blender, quickly break up the ice crystals until they are evenly distributed throughout the mixture. Return to freezer. Repeat the process 3 to 4 more times, every 30 to 40 minutes, or until a

KIWI-RASPBERRY FRAPPE

4   medium kiwi, peeled
1   pound fresh raspberries, hulled
1   to 2 tablespoon granulated sugar
½   teaspoon lemon juice

2½ cups sparkling water
Crushed ice
Thin slices of peeled kiwi

Step 1.   Coarsely chop the kiwi and place in tall pitcher. Add the raspberries, sugar, lemon juice and sparkling water.

Step 2.   Using a hand blender, pureé the fruit mixture until smooth and refrigerate until ready to use.

Step 3.   Place some crushed ice in a goblet or tall glass. Pour fruit mixture over the ice and garnish with a kiwi slice to serve.

Yield: 4 to 6 servings

VARIATIONS

Mango Frappé: Place **¼ cup grenadine**, **1¼ cups fresh orange juice**, **¾ cup fresh lime juice**, **1¼ cups mango juice drink** and **1 cup sparkling water** in a tall pitcher. Using a hand blender, process mixture until smooth. Pour over ice and garnish with a **sprig of fresh mint**. **Yield: 4 to 6 servings**

Cherry-Orange Frappé: Place **1¼ cups (11 oz. can) Mandarin orange sections**, **1 cup cherry juice**, **2 cups ginger ale**, **½ cup granulated sugar** and **1½ cups fresh orange juice** in a tall pitcher. Using a hand blender, process mixture until smooth. Pour over crushed ice and serve with a mini-skewer of assorted fruit. **Yield: 4 to 6 servings**

FROZEN "WATERMELON" BOMBE

Vegetable oil

1 quart purchased mint (or pistachio) ice cream, slightly softened

1 quart Buttermilk Ice Cream (page 148)

1 quart Strawberry Sherbet (page 140) or purchased raspberry sherbet

¼ cup dark chocolate morsels

Step 1. To prepare mold, lightly oil an 8-cup stainless steel bowl with vegetable oil and place in the freezer for about 10 minutes to chill.

Step 2. To assemble watermelon, remove the bowl from the freezer. Using a rubber spatula, spread the entire inside of the bowl evenly with a ¾-inch-thick layer of mint ice cream. Return bowl to freezer for a few minutes and refreeze ice cream, enough to maintain workability.

Step 3. Remove from freezer and cover layer of ice cream with a sheet of plastic wrap. Press down lightly on the ice cream to remove any air pockets and then return mold to freezer for one hour or until firmly set.

Step 4. Meanwhile, soften the buttermilk ice cream slightly. Remove mold from freezer and pull off the plastic wrap. Spread a ½-inch-thick layer of buttermilk ice cream over the mint-flavored layer until evenly covered. Cover with plastic wrap and freeze for at least an hour or until firmly set.

Step 5. Meanwhile, soften the sherbet slightly and transfer to a bowl. Add the chocolate, stirring until the morsels (or watermelon "seeds") are evenly dispersed in the sherbet.

Step 6. Remove mold from the freezer and pull off plastic wrap. Spoon in the chocolate/sherbet mixture, fill the cavity. Cover with plastic and return to the freezer for 3 to 4 hours or until firmly set. (You may freeze for as long as 3 days before serving.)

Step 7. To unmold bombe, remove the plastic wrap and place mold in a bowl of hot water for 2 to 4 seconds—just enough to loosen the bombe from the sides and bottom of the mold. Invert onto a chilled platter, cover and return to freezer for 15 to 20 minutes or until the outside of the bombe has set.

Step 8. To serve, dip a slicing knife into hot water, wipe dry and then cut into slices to serve.

Yield: 6 to 8 servings

FROZEN CHERRY SOUFFLE
WITH COFFEE CREME

Parchment paper (or aluminum foil)

Soufflé

2 pounds fresh cherries

1¼ cups granulated sugar

½ cup water

6 large egg whites, room temperature

1 cup heavy cream

1 tablespoon kirsch or other
   cherry-flavored liqueur

Sauce

½ cup whole coffee beans

½ cup heavy cream

½ cup milk

2 egg yolks

2 tablespoons granulated sugar

1 tablespoon coffee-flavored liqueur
   (Kahlúa)

Extra whole fresh cherries (optional)

Step 1. To prepare soufflé dish, cut a sheet of parchment paper (or foil) about 24-inches long. Fold into a 3 to 4-inch-wide strip. Wrap the strip around the outer edge of a 1-quart soufflé dish and secure with butcher's twine or tape, creating a 2 to 3-inch-high "collar" that extends up above the sides of the dish. Set aside.

Step 2. To prepare soufflé, wash, stem and pit the cherries (enough to make 4 cups) and chop into small pieces. Place cherries and ½ cup of the sugar in a heavy, 2-quart saucepan over low heat. Cook, uncovered and stirring often, for 8 to 10 minutes or until cherries are soft and their liquid thickens somewhat. Remove from heat, transfer to a large bowl and cool.

Step 3. Meanwhile, place ½ cup of the remaining sugar in a heavy, 1-quart saucepan. Add the water and cook over medium heat, stirring constantly, until the sugar dissolves.

Step 4. Continue to boil until syrup reaches 238°F (called the *soft-ball stage*) on a candy thermometer.

Step 5. Meanwhile, place the egg whites in a large mixing bowl. Beat to a soft-peak stage, while adding the remaining ¼ cup sugar.

Step 6. While continuing to beat, add the syrup in a slow, steady stream and beat until the mixture is light and fluffy, somewhat cool to the touch and becomes a meringue. Set aside.

Step 7. Combine the cream and the kirsch in a large bowl and whip cream to a stiff-peak consistency.

Step 8. Temper the cherry mixture by folding in about one-half of the meringue. This helps to lighten the texture. Now, fold in the remaining meringue. Use a rubber spatula in a lifting-type motion to combine, taking care not to deflate the meringue by over-working.

Step 9. Gently fold the cherry/meringue mixture into the whipped cream using the same lifting-type motion as described in Step 8.

Step 10. Spoon into the prepared soufflé dish and place in the freezer for 1 to 2 hours or until firmly set.

Step 11. Meanwhile, to prepare sauce, slightly crush (or *bruise*) the coffee beans using a rolling pin and place in a heavy, 1-quart saucepan. Add the cream and milk and place over moderate heat until scalded. Remove, cover and allow beans to steep for about 30 minutes.

Step 12. Meanwhile, whisk the egg yolks and sugar together for 4 to 6 minutes or until the sugar dissolves and the mixture is thick and pale-yellow in color.

Step 13. Reheat the coffee/cream mixture in a sauce pan. Temper the egg mixture by adding one-fourth of the hot cream to the eggs, whisking vigorously to combine. Return tempered egg mixture back to saucepan. Whisk gently over low heat until the mixture thickens and coats the back of a spoon.

Step 14. Pour sauce through a fine mesh strainer and stir in liqueur until combined.

Step 15. To serve, remove soufflé from freezer, garnish with reserved whole cherries (if desired) and offer coffee crème as an accompaniment.

Yield: 6 to 8 servings

PHILADELPHIA-STYLE
ORANGE BUTTERMILK ICE CREAM

Ice Cream

1   small orange
1   quart buttermilk
¾   cup granulated sugar
¼   cup orange-flavored liqueur
     (Grand Marnier or Cointreau)
½   teaspoon almond extract

Sauce

1⅓   pounds of dark baker's chocolate
1   cup heavy cream
½   teaspoon vanilla extract
1   ounce orange-flavored liqueur
1   ounce almond-flavored liqueur
     (Amaretto)

Toasted sliced almonds (optional)

Step 1.   To prepare ice cream, use a zester to remove only the colored portion of the peel from the orange. You should have about 2 tablespoons of zest. Set aside.

Step 2.   In a large mixing bowl, combine the buttermilk, sugar, liqueur, almond extract and zest. Whisk or process with a hand blender until the sugar dissolves and the mixture is well blended.

Step 3.   Transfer the mixture to the canister of an ice cream maker and freeze according to the manufacturer's instructions. Cover and store in the freezer until ready to serve.

Step 4.   Meanwhile, to prepare sauce, place the block of chocolate on a cutting board. Starting at one corner of the chocolate block and using the blade of a chef's knife like a paper cutter, shave down through the chocolate, cutting off small pieces at a time.

Step 5.   As you whittle away each corner, rotate the block of chocolate in order to work on another corner. Continue shaving until all the chocolate is in small, similar-sized pieces. Set aside.

Step 6.   Pour the cream into a heavy, 3-quart saucepan. Add the vanilla, orange liqueur and almond liqueur. Place over moderate heat until cream begins to scald or reaches 180° to 190°F.

Step 7.   Remove from heat. Add the chocolate pieces and whisk for 2 to 3 minutes or until the chocolate sauce is satiny, smooth and homogenous. You should see no whisps of unincorporated cream or any lumps of chocolate remaining.

Step 8. To serve, place one or two scoops of ice cream in a dessert glass, spoon over some warm chocolate sauce and garnish with a sprinkling of almonds, if desired.

Yield: 4 to 6 servings

VARIATION

Chocolate Buttermilk Ice Cream: Chop ⅛ **pound baking (unsweetened) chocolate** and ⅛ **pound semi-sweet chocolate** into small pieces, as described above. Melt in the top of a double boiler or over a bain marie. Combine **1 quart buttermilk**, **¾ cup granulated sugar**, **2 ounces chocolate-flavored liqueur (Crème de Cacao)**, and **½ teaspoon vanilla extract** in a bowl. Stir in the melted chocolates until blended. Transfer the mixture to the canister of an ice cream maker and freeze according to manufacturer's directions. **Yield: 4 to 6 servings**

INDIVIDUAL BAKED ALASKA
WITH RASPBERRY SAUCE

Sauce

1   pint fresh raspberries (or frozen raspberries without syrup)

½   teaspoon cornstarch

Ice Cream Base

6   thin slices poundcake, cut ¼-inch thick

1   quart purchased Neopolitan ice cream

Meringue

½   cup egg whites

⅔   cup granulated sugar

¼   cup light corn syrup

¼   cup water

¼   cup powdered sugar

¼   cup sour cream

    Heavy cream

Step 1.   To prepare sauce, purée the raspberries using a hand blender or food processor until smooth. Pour through a fine mesh strainer into a heavy, 1-quart saucepan.

Step 2.   In a small bowl, combine the cornstarch with a small amount of raspberry purée until blended. Return cornstarch mixture to saucepan, stirring to combine. Cook sauce over medium heat for 1 to 2 minutes or until cornstarch taste is lost and sauce thickens.

Step 3.   To assemble ice cream bases, line a baking pan with a sheet of parchment paper. Using a 2½ to 3-inch round cookie cutter (or coffee mug), cut a circle out of each slice of poundcake. Place the cake circles on the sheetpan. Place a small scoop (2 to 3 ounces) of ice cream in the center of each cake round, taking care to leave a small margin of cake visible all the way around. Place in the freezer while preparing the meringue.

Step 4.   To prepare meringue, place the sugar, corn syrup and water in a heavy, 1-quart saucepan over moderate heat. Bring to a boil and cook until syrup reaches 230°F (*thread stage*) on a candy thermometer.

Step 5.   Meanwhile, place the egg whites in a deep mixing bowl. Continue to boil the syrup, and at the same time start whipping the egg whites on high speed. When the syrup reaches 247°F (*firm-ball stage*), lower the speed of the mixer and pour the syrup, in a slow steady stream, into the egg whites. Return to high speed and continue whipping until the meringue reaches a stiff-peak consistency (called an *Italian meringue*).

Step 6.   Transfer the meringue in a pastry bag fitted with a No. 4 plain tip. Remove ice cream bases from the freezer. The next step is to create a "meringue beehive" by piping a continuous line of meringue starting at the bottom edge of the cake base and ending up on top of the scoop of ice cream.

Step 7. Starting at the edge of each base, pipe a ring of meringue around the scoop of ice cream so that it completely covers the exposed margin of cake. Continue to encircle the scoop of ice cream with a continuous line of meringue. Make sure as you add a circle of meringue that it rests on top of the previous one. Finish with a small circle at the top of the ice cream. Repeat with remaining ice cream bases. Return meringues to the freezer.

Step 8. Meanwhile, to decorate plate, thin the sour cream with enough heavy cream until it equals the consistency of the raspberry sauce. Pour the decorating cream into a plastic squeeze bottle with a narrow tip. Choose an over-sized plate for presentation, allowing enough room for the sauce and its decoration.

Step 9. Place a heaping tablespoon (or so) of sauce in the center of each plate. Tilt the plate slightly, in each direction, to spread the sauce evenly. Use just enough sauce to thinly cover the plate—you should still be able to see the bottom of the plate through the sauce.

Step 10. Squeeze out a "ring" of the decorating cream (at least 4 inches in diameter) in the raspberry sauce. Make sure that the ring is about an inch in from the rim of the sauce. Drag a toothpick, in a continuous, corkscrew-like motion, through the circle of decorating cream to create a pattern. Repeat procedure with remaining plates.

Step 11. To serve, preheat the oven to broil. Remove baking sheet of meringues from the freezer. Spoon the sugar into a fine mesh strainer. Tapping the edges of the strainer, dust the top of each meringue with a sprinkling of powdered sugar.

Step 12. Place the baking sheet in the preheated oven *but leave the door open*. Broil for 30 to 45 seconds or just until meringue begins to brown. Remove from oven and place each on a decorated plate to serve.

Yield: 6 servings

CHEESECAKE SOUFFLE
WITH MANGO GINGER SAUCE

Sauce
1   small piece fresh ginger (½-inch)
½   cup fresh orange juice
1½   pounds fresh mangoes
2   to 3 tablespoons fresh lime juice
2   tablespoons honey

Softened butter
Granulated sugar

Soufflé
4   large eggs
2   tablespoons granulated sugar
6   ounces cream cheese, softened
2   teaspoons lemon zest
1   teaspoon vanilla extract
1   tablespoon fresh lemon juice

Confectioners' sugar

Step 1.   To prepare sauce, peel the ginger and cut into julienne strips. Heat orange juice in a heavy, 1-quart saucepan until scalded. Add the ginger, remove from heat, cover and set aside to steep for 30 minutes. Pour through a fine strainer to remove the ginger. Set juice aside.

Step 2.   Peel mango, cut into pieces and place in the bowl of a food processor fitted with a metal blade. Add the lime juice, orange juice and honey and process until smooth. Set aside.

Step 3.   To prepare soufflé, preheat oven to 425°F. Lighty butter and dust the inside of six 4-ounce ramekins with sugar. Place on a baking sheet and set aside.

Step 4.   Separate the eggs, placing the yolks in a large bowl and whites in a medium bowl.

Step 5.   Add the sugar to the egg yolks and whisk for 3 to 5 minutes or until the sugar has dissolved and the mixture becomes thick, pale yellow in color, and forms a ribbon-like design when mixture is lifted and allowed to fall back into the bowl. (This is called the *ribbon stage*.)

Step 6.   Beat the cream cheese briefly if it is not soft and pliable. Then add it to the egg yolk mixture and incorporate gently, making sure that no lumps remain.

Step 7.   Add lemon zest and vanilla and continue to beat until mixture is fully incorporated.

Step 8.   Meanwhile, whip the egg whites for 6 to 8 minutes or until they reach soft-peak consistency. Add lemon juice and continue to whip, slowly adding 1 teaspoon sugar, until the whites reach a medium peak.

Step 9.   Before folding the mixtures together, temper the egg whites by folding in about one-third of the cream cheese mixture.

Step 10.   Using a lifting motion, quickly fold in remaining egg whites just until incorporated. Speed is critical here as any delay causes whites to curdle and makes incorporation difficult.

Step 11.   Divide mixture between the six prepared ramekins and bake in the preheated oven for 15 to 20 minutes or until the sides and top turn light brown.

Step 12.   Remove from oven and dust tops with sifted powdered sugar. Serve immediately offering mango sauce as an accompaniment.

Yield: 6 servings

FRESH FRUIT TART
WITH APRICOT GLAZE

Short Dough
7 ounces butter
⅓ cup (3 oz.) granulated sugar
1 large egg
¼ teaspoon vanilla extract
2½ cups (9 oz.) all-purpose flour
Bread flour

Parchment paper
Dried beans (or pie weights)

Pastry Cream
1 cup milk
¼ cup (2 oz.) granulated sugar
3 tablespoons cornstarch
1 large egg

Pinch of salt
¼ teaspoon vanilla extract

Glaze
¼ cup apricot jam
¼ cup (2 oz.) granulated sugar
¼ cup water

Fruit
10 to 12 large strawberries, hulled
4 or 5 plums
2 medium oranges
2 kiwis

Whipped cream
Sprigs of mint

Step 1. To make dough, place the butter, sugar, egg and vanilla in a large bowl. Using two forks or a spoon, mix just until combined. Slowly add the flour, mixing briefly.

Step 2. Continue to mix the dough by hand, in a kneading-style motion, until the dough is smooth. Remove dough from the bowl and flatten into a disk; cover with plastic wrap and refrigerate for 30 minutes to 1 hour.

Step 3. To make pastry cream, scald the milk (180° to 190°F) in a heavy, 1-quart saucepan over medium heat. While the milk is heating, place the sugar, cornstarch, salt and egg in a bowl and mix thoroughly. Add vanilla until combined.

Step 4. Slowly, pour in about 2 tablespoons of hot milk into the sugar mixture, whisking constantly and rapidly. (This is to *temper* the eggs. You don't want them to coagulate when they are added to the hot milk mixture.)

Step 5. Return the tempered egg mixture back into the saucepan, whisking constantly and rapidly. Place over medium heat and cook, stirring constantly with a whisk (or hand blender) until the mixture comes to a slow boil and begins to thicken.

Step 6. Place a sheet of wax paper directly on top of the pastry cream to prevent a skin from forming. Allow to come to room temperature. (If made in advance, chill in refrigerator for up to 3 days.)

Step 7.   To prepare tart shell, preheat the oven to 375°F. Remove dough from refrigerator and knead for a few minutes until soft and pliable (no cracks should appear on the surface of the dough). Flatten dough into a disk and place on a flat surface. Dust the surface with a small amount of bread flour.

Step 8.   Roll out the dough to a thickness of ¼-inch . You should have a circle about 12-inches in diameter. Transfer dough to a 9-inch tart pan with a removable bottom. Gently press the dough down into the pan, fitting it in and around the fluted edges. Place the rolling pin on the edge of the tart pan. Using it as a cutter, roll the pin over all the edges of the pan to cut off the excess dough.

Step 9.   Place a sheet of parchment paper in the tart pan. Pour in enough dried beans (or pie weights) to almost fill the pan. This will keep the dough from shifting during baking.

Step 10. Place in the preheated oven and bake for 15 to 18 minutes or until the edges of the crust begin to turn golden brown. Remove dried beans and parchment paper. Return shell to oven for about 5 minutes longer or until bottom is also golden brown. Remove from oven and set aside to cool.

Step 11. Meanwhile, to make apricot glaze, combine jam, sugar and water in a heavy, 1-quart saucepan over medium heat. Bring to a boil, stirring constantly to avoid burning. Continue cooking and stirring, for 6 to 8 minutes longer, or until glaze thickens and when tested using the back of two spoons, can be pulled into a ¼-inch-long thread (called the *tread stage*). Remove from heat.

Step 12. To fill tart, brush the warm apricot glaze over the bottom and sides of the baked shell, reserving the remaining glaze for the topping. Spread the custard evenly into the tart pan, taking care that the cream fills no more than three-fourths of the shell. You need to leave room for the fruit.

Step 13. To cut fruit, thinly slice the strawberries and the plums. Peel and segment the oranges. Peel, cut in half and thinly slice the kiwi. Beginning at the outer edge, arrange most of the strawberry slices in a circle all the way around tart. Next arrange a circle of orange segments, followed by a circle of plums and then kiwi.

Step 14. Place two slices of kiwi in the center of the tart. Arrange the remaining strawberries in the uncovered area. When the custard is covered with fruit, brush all the fruit with the remaining glaze. (If the glaze is too thick, you may need to reheat it slightly.)

Step 15. To serve, cut tart into wedges and garnish with a dollop of whipped cream and a sprig of mint.

Yield: 6 to 8 servings

MENDOCINO POACHED PEAR
ON CHOCOLATE WITH ALMOND-PEAR SAUCE

4   cups water
1   tablespoon fresh lemon juice
4   Bosch pears with stems

Poaching Liquid
5   cups water
1   to 2 tablespoons fresh lemon juice
¼   cup granulated sugar
1   teaspoon vanilla extract
4   whole cloves
1   cinnamon stick

1   bottle (4 cups) Zinfandel

Sauce
1   to 1½ cups water
1   tablespoon fresh lemon juice
2   tablespoons almond-flavored liqueur (Amaretto)
¼   cup granulated sugar
2   tablespoons cornstarch

2   ounces dark baker's chocolate
    Fresh mint sprigs

Step 1.   In a large bowl, combine the water and lemon juice (called *acidulated water*). Cut the pears in half lengthwise, taking care to leave the stem attached to one half of each pear. Peel the *stemmed* pear halves with a vegetable peeler. Try to maintain the contour of the pear half as you work.

Step 2.   Place the *stemmed* pear halves in the bowl of acidulated water to prevent them from turning brown and set aside until later.

Step 3.   To make poaching liquid, pour the 5 cups of water into a heavy, 4-quart saucepan. Add the lemon juice, sugar, vanilla, cloves and cinnamon stick. Add the *stemless* pear halves.

Step 4.   Place pan over moderate heat and bring to a boil. Reduce heat and cover pan with a smaller-sized lid making sure that it rests directly on the pears. The smaller lid keeps the pears submerged, thus guaranteeing even cooking. Simmer, for 10 to 15 minutes or until pears are soft to the touch.

Step 5.   Remove cooked *stemless* pears with a slotted spoon and set aside for finishing the sauce. Pour off all but 2 cups of the poaching liquid and add the wine. Arrange the *stemmed* pear halves in the liquid, re-cover with the smaller-sized lid and bring to a boil over moderate heat. Reduce heat and simmer for 5 to 10 minutes or until pears are soft to the touch.

Step 6.   Remove pan from the heat and set aside, allowing pears to steep in the poaching liquid for at least 12 hours or overnight. The Zinfandel will cause the pears to take on a beautiful rosey-red color.

Step 7.   Meanwhile, to prepare the sauce, use a melon baller to remove the cores from the *stemless* pears. Using a hand blender or food processor, purée the pears until smooth. Add the water, lemon juice, Amaretto and sugar and continue to process until blended.

Step 8.   In a small bowl, stir together about ¼ cup of the pear purée with the cornstarch until combined. Stir the cornstarch mixture back into the purée. Transfer purée to a heavy, 1-quart saucepan and place over medium heat. Simmer for 2 to 3 minutes, stirring often, until the cornstarch has cooked and the sauce begins to thicken. Remove and set aside to cool. (If made in advance, cover and chill in the refrigerator for up to 3 days.)

Step 9.   To prepare chocolate, break up the chocolate and place in a double boiler (or *bain-marie*) over low heat until melted. Transfer to a plastic squeeze bottle (or small parchment paper *cornet*). You are trying to keep the chocolate liquid enough to "paint" a pattern on the dessert plate. If the chocolate begins to harden, set the plastic squeeze bottle in a pan of warm water just until chocolate melts again.

Step 10. To "paint" the plate with chocolate, place a dessert plate on a piece of parchment paper for easy clean-up. (If using a paper *cornet*, cut a small opening in the tip.)

Step 11. Using a continuous motion, pipe thin lines of chocolate, ¼-inch to ½-inch apart, horizontally across the top half of each plate. For a better appearance, start piping the chocolate *over* the parchment paper, slightly off to one side of the rim of the plate. Pipe horizonally all the way across the plate, continuing off the opposite rim. Set the plates aside for the chocolate to harden.

Step 12. To assemble, remove the *stemmed* pears from the poaching liquid and blot dry. Using a melon baller, carefully remove each core. You will notice how the inside of the pear is still light yellow in color.

Step 13. Starting ½-inch below the stem, cut each pear half (vertically) into thin slices, taking care to see that the slices remain attached at the stem. You should be able to flair out each into a fan shape.

Step 14. Place the pear half, cut-side-down, so that it overlaps onto the chocolate. Fan out the slices in a decorative way. Spoon a small amount of sauce onto the unlined (without chocolate) portion of the plate and garnish with a sprig of mint to serve.

Yield: 8 servings (Pictured on page 143.)

TRUFFLED BANANA FRITTERS
WITH KIWI & TANGERINE COULIS

Coulis

1   cup tangerine juice
1   teaspoon sugar
1   tablespoon arrowroot
2   tablespoons orange-flavored liqueur
    (Grand Marnier)

Purée

4   kiwis
1   to 2 tablespoons sugar
1   tablespoon lime juice

½   cup heavy cream
¾   cup chopped dark chocolate
¾   cup chopped milk chocolate
4   ripe bananas
½   cup hazelnuts, toasted, peeled and
    crushed fine
12 spring roll (or egg roll) wrappers

    Vegetable oil
½   cup confectioners' sugar

Step 1.   To make tangerine coulis, combine tangerine juice, arrowroot and sugar in a saucepan and heat to desired thickness. Stir in the liqueur. Adjust sweetness as necessary.

Step 2.   To make kiwi purée, peel kiwis and purée in a food processor in short off-on bursts to prevent seeds from breaking (thereby changing the color of the coulis). Add sugar and lime juice to taste.

Step 3.   Place the cream in a heavy, 1-quart saucepan. Place over moderate heat until cream begins to scald or reaches 180° to 190°F.

Step 4.   Remove from heat. Add the dark and milk chocolates and whisk for 2 to 3 minutes or until the mixture is satiny, smooth and homogenous. You should see no whisps of unincorporated cream or any lumps of chocolate remaining. (This is called a *ganache*.) Transfer to a bowl and cool.

Step 5.   Peel the bananas and split them in half lengthwise. Then cut each half into thirds. You should have 24 pieces.

Step 6.   Place the ganache in a piping bag and using a plain tip, pipe a layer of the ganache down the center of 12 of the pieces. Sprinkle the top of the piped chocolate with toasted hazelnuts.

Step 7.   "Sandwich" the banana pieces back together, using a half with ganache and a half without. Wrap each re-assembled banana section into a springroll wrapper exactly as you would wrap a springroll. (The directions are on the package.)

Step 8.   Using your fingertips, moisten the outer edge of the spring roll wrapper with water to seal the fritter together. Repeat with remaining fritters.

Step 9.   Meanwhile, pour oil into a deep-sided, heavy saucepan and heat to a temperature of 375°F. When oil is hot, lower the fritters into the oil, a few at a time, and deep-fry to golden brown. Remove fritters with a slotted spoon and drain on paper towels.

Step 10. Dust each fritter with powdered sugar. Pour some tangerine coulis and kiwi purée on a dessert plate. Arrange a fritter on top to serve.

Yield: 6 servings (Pictured on page 142.)

CHOCOLATE BREAD PUDDING
WITH BERRY SAUCE & ALMOND TUILES

Sauce

¼ pound fresh raspberries

¼ pound fresh strawberries

2 to 3 tablespoons granulated sugar

1 tablespoon fresh lemon juice

1 tablespoon cherry-flavored liqueur
(Kirsch)

Tuiles

1¾ tablespoons sweet butter

¾ cup granulated sugar

1 tablespoon vanilla extract

4 egg whites

¼ cup sifted all-purpose flour

1¾ cups ground blanched almonds

Pudding

¼ loaf French bread, cut into 1-inch cubes

1 cup heavy cream

2 ounces bittersweet chocolate

1 ounce unsweetened chocolate

3 ounces sweet butter

3 large eggs

⅓ cup granulated sugar

½ cup ground almonds

Softened butter

Fresh raspberries (optional)

Step 1. To make sauce, combine raspberries, strawberries and sugar in food processor fitted with a metal blade. Process until smooth and puréed. Pour through a fine strainer to remove the seeds.

Step 2. Stir in the lemon juice and liqueur. Cover and store refrigerated in air tight container for up to a week.

Step 3. To make tuiles, beat together the butter, sugar and vanilla for 3 to 5 minutes or until soft and well blended. Add the egg whites and continue to beat, scraping the sides of the bowl as you work.

Step 4. Fold in the flour and the almond meal until batter is well combined. Cover and refrigerate for at least 2 hour or overnight.

Step 5. To bake tuiles, preheat the oven 325°F. Place about 2 teaspoons of the batter on a non-stick baking sheet without sides and using the back of the spoon, gently spread batter into a circle about 6 inches in diameter. Batter should be uniformly thin—enough to see through but not so thin that holes appear through the surface. Repeat with more batter, placing another circle (or two) about 2 inches apart on the baking sheet. (Note: If using a baking pan with sides, turn pan over and bake on the back side instead.)

Step 6. Place baking sheet in the preheated oven and bake for 5 to 8 minutes or until cookie just turns golden brown. Leaving baking sheet in the oven, quickly remove cookies (one at a time) with a metal spatula and roll them up, cigar-style. Repeat with remaining batter until all the tuiles are baked and rolled. Set aside.

Step 7. To prepare pudding, preheat oven to 350°F. Place the bread cubes and cream in a large bowl and soak for 30 minutes.

Step 8. Meanwhile, chop the chocolate in small pieces and place in the top of a double boiler over low heat until melted. Keep warm.

Step 9. Separate the eggs, reserving whites for later use. Cream together the butter, sugar and egg yolks in a large bowl until well blended. Add the soaked bread cubes, almonds and melted chocolate.

Step 10 Whip the reserved egg whites to a soft-peak consistency and using a rubber spatula, fold egg whites into the mixture.

Step 11. Lightly butter the inside of a 2-quart soufflé dish. Pour in the batter. Place soufflé dish in a roasting pan and set the pan in the oven. Carefully, pour in enough hot water to come at least half-way up the sides of the terrine. (The water temperature should be around 170°F.)

Step 12. Bake in preheated oven for 40 to 50 minutes. Remove and allow to cool for 10 minutes.

Step 13. Place a few spoonfuls of pudding in a dessert dish, garnish with fresh raspberries and offer the berry sauce and tuiles as accompaniments.

Yield: 6 servings (Pictured on page 141.)

CHOCOLATE MOCHA
INSIDE/OUT CAKE

Parchment paper

Spongecakes

2 egg whites
10 ounces almond paste
12 large eggs, separated
1⅓ cups (10 oz.) granulated sugar
1 teaspoon vanilla extract
2¾ cups (8 oz.) cake flour, sifted
⅔ cup (1 oz.) cocoa powder

Buttercreams

1 pound unsalted butter, softened
5 ounces margarine, softened

1 cup egg whites
1 pound granulated sugar
1 teaspoon vanilla extract
6 ounces melted dark chocolate
¼ cup espresso coffee

¼ cup coffee-flavored liqueur (Kahlúa)
⅓ cup water
½ cup toasted sliced almonds
Dark chocolate shavings

Cardboard cake rounds
Pastry bag fitted with a No. 4 plain tip

Step 1. To prepare sponges, preheat the oven to 375°F. Line the bottom of two 10-inch round cake pans with parchment paper and set aside.

Step 2. Place the 2 egg whites in a large bowl and gradually work in the almond paste to make a smooth mixture.

Step 3. In a mixing bowl, beat together the 12 egg yolks with ½-cup of the sugar. Beat for 2 to 3 minutes or until the sugar has dissolved and the mixture becomes thick, pale yellow in color, and forms a ribbon-like design when mixture is lifted and allowed to fall back into the bowl. (This is called the *ribbon stage*). Add the vanilla.

Step 4. Gradually, stir the egg yolk mixture into the almond paste and set aside.

Step 5. In another bowl, whip the remaining 12 egg whites until foamy. Gradually add the remaining 2¼-cups of sugar and whip until the stiff-peak consistency is reached. Carefully fold the whipped egg whites into the yolk mixture.

Step 6. Gently, fold in the flour, using a spatula to mix the ingredients and taking care not to deflate the egg whites. Pour *a little less than half* of the batter into one of the 10-inch cake pans. Set aside.

Step 7. Sift the cocoa powder on top of the remaining batter and fold in just to combine; *do not* overmix. Pour the chocolate batter into the other prepared cake pan. Place in the preheated oven and bake for about 25 minutes or until the top springs back when pressed lightly in the center. Remove and set aside to cool. When the sponges have cooled, cut around the sides

Step 8. To prepare buttercream, beat together the soft butter and margarine in a small bowl.

Step 9. Combine the egg whites and sugar in a mixing bowl. Place the bowl over simmering water and whisk constantly for about 3 minutes or until the sugar is dissolved. *Be careful not to cook the egg whites.*

Step 10. Remove the egg whites from the heat and whip with an electric mixer until the mixture is cool and has formed stiff peaks. Lower the speed of the mixer and add the vanilla extract. With the mixer on low speed, gradually whip in the butter mixture.

Step 11. Divide the buttercream (about 6 cups total) into two bowls. Combine half of the buttercream with the melted dark chocolate and the other half with the espresso, stirring well to combine. Set aside.

Step 12. To assemble cake, cut the almond spongecake into three even layers, each about ¼-inch thick. Reserve the top layer for another use as it will not be used in this recipe. Cut the chocolate spongecake into three even layers, ¼-inch thick. (You should now have 5 thin layers–two almond sponges and three chocolate sponges.)

Step 13. Place one of the chocolate layers, cut-side-up, on a cardboard cake round. Combine the Kahlúa and water in a small bowl. Moisten the cake by brushing some of this mixture on top. Spread a layer of coffee-flavored buttercream, about ¼-inch-thick, on the chocolate layer.

Step 14. Place an almond spongecake layer on top of the coffee buttercream. Moisten the almond sponge by brushing it with some of the Kahlúa/water, then spread a layer of coffee buttercream, about ¼-inch thick, on top.

Step 15. Repeat Steps 13 and 14 again, adding one more chocolate spongecake layer and one more almond spongecake layer, taking care to brush with the Kahlúa mixture each time before spreading the buttercream. You should end with an almond layer on top. Do not brush any Kahlúa on this one. (Note: You still have a chocolate layer left which will be used later.) Chill the cake for about 15 minutes or until the buttercream is set.

Step 16. To cut the cake, dip a serrated knife in hot water and wipe dry. Cut a cone-shaped section from the center of the cake, about 8 inches wide at the top and 2 inches wide at the bottom. Think of it as the "crater" of a volcano. Place your hand flat on top of the cone-shaped wedge and, using the knife or a spatula to remove the wedge, invert it onto your hand. Place the cone-shaped wedge, flat-side-down, on a cardboard cake round. Set aside.

Step 17. Working inside the "crater" or hole of the cake, spread a layer of chocolate buttercream, about ¼-inch thick, lining the inside of the "crater."

continued on page 164

Step 18. Place the reserved chocolate spongecake layer flat on top of the cake (suspended over the hole). Place a cardboard cake round on top and invert the cake so that the new chocolate layer is now on the bottom. Set the cake aside at room temperature (covered) for about 30 minutes to soften the buttercream in between the layers.

Step 19. You are now going to reconstruct the "crater" by replacing the cone-shaped cut-out that you have set aside. Gently press the top of the cake down into the "crater" so that the top touches the bottom. You have now created a new "crater" in the cake.

Step 20. Spread a layer of chocolate buttercream, about ¼-inch thick, to line the inside of the "crater." Replace the cone-shaped cut-out. Trim off the sides of the cake to its original shape.

Step 21. Spread the remaining chocolate buttercream on the top and sides of the cake. Press in the toasted almond slices around the sides of the cake.

Step 22. Place the remaining coffee buttercream in a pastry bag fitted with a No. 4 plain tip. Starting at the center of the cake and working outward, pipe the buttercream in a circular fashion on the top of the cake until completely covered. Garnish with a sprinkling of chocolate shavings.

Yield: About 12 servings

GLAZED SEASONAL FRUIT

2 pounds (*total*) strawberries, oranges
   and apples
   Lemon juice

Parchment paper

Syrup
1 cup water
2 pounds sugar
2 ounces corn syrup

Step 1.   To prepare the fruit, rinse the strawberries, leaving the stems attached, and pat dry. Slice off the ends of the oranges, leaving the skin on, and then cut into eighths. Trim off and discard the center membrane of each piece. Cut the apples into eighths. Remove the cores and rub each piece with some lemon juice to prevent discoloration.

Step 2.   To prepare syrup, combine the water, sugar and corn syrup in a heavy, 3-quart saucepan over moderate heat. Bring to a boil. This next procedure is very important. You want to prevent sugar crystals from forming on the inside of the pan, which would render it useless for glazing fruit. As the temperature of the syrup rises, use a pastry brush and some water to brush down the sides of the pan. (This is the exposed pan just above the surface of the boiling syrup.)

Step 3.   Continue to boil the syrup, while brushing continuously, until the temperature reaches 300° to 310°F on the candy thermometer (called the *hard-crack stage*). You can test for the hard-crack stage by placing a drop of the boiling sugar-syrup into cold water. It should shatter into hard, brittle threads when immersed.

Step 4.   Remove pan from heat. To stop the cooking process at the hard-crack stage, place the pan in cold (or ice) water. When the bubbling stop rising from the bottom, remove the pan.

Step 5.   Line a baking pan with a piece of parchment paper.

Step 6.   To glaze fruit, check to see that the temperature of the syrup is about 280°F. Carefully, hand-dip the strawberries, one at a time while holding onto their stem, into the sugar. Take care not to get your fingers close to the hot syrup. As each strawberry is dipped, place on the parchment to dry. Holding them by the rind, dip the orange pieces one-half of the way into the syrup until coated. Repeat as directed with the apple wedges.

Step 7.   When completely hardened, arrange fruit on a display plate to serve.

Yield: 4 to 6 servings

Note: Sugar is very sensitive to the presence of water. Fruits that can be glazed most successfully are those with skins such as grapes, strawberries and cherries, or sliced fruits with low moisture content such as bananas, apples and pineapples. Excessively juicy fruits will not survive long after being dipped.

ACADEMY LIGHT TRUFFLES
WITH PISTACHIOS

Simple Syrup
1   quart water
2   cups granulated sugar
2   cups light corn syrup

Ganache
2¼ pounds white chocolate
6   ounces cocoa butter

1   ounce pistachios, skinned
1¾ cups heavy cream
6   ounces praline paste
6   ounces unsalted butter, soft
¼   cup confectioners' sugar

Parchment paper

1   pound white baker's chocolate

Step 1.   To make simple syrup, combine the water, sugar and the corn syrup in a heavy, 2-quart saucepan. Bring to a boil over moderate heat, stirring until sugar is dissolved. Set aside to cool, taking care to skim off any impurities that may have accumulated on the surface.

Step 2.   When cool, place in covered container and store for up to 10 days.

Step 3.   To prepare ganache, place the block of chocolate on a cutting board. Starting at one corner of the chocolate block and using the blade of a chef's knife like a paper cutter, shave down through the chocolate, cutting off small pieces at a time. As you whittle away each corner, rotate the block of chocolate in order to work on another corner. Continue shaving until all the chocolate is in small, similar-sized pieces. Set aside.

Step 4.   Cut the cocoa butter into small pieces and set aside.

Step 5.   Pour the cream into a heavy, 3-quart saucepan. Place over moderate heat until cream begins to scald or reaches 180° to 190°F.

Step 6.   Remove from heat. Add the chocolate and cocoa butter pieces and whisk for 2 to 3 minutes or until the mixture is satiny, smooth and homogenous. You should see no whisps of un-incorporated cream or any lumps of chocolate remaining. This mixture is now called a *ganache*. Transfer the ganache to a bowl and cool to a temperature of 85° to 87°F.

Step 7.   Meanwhile, blend the praline paste and butter together using a hand mixer until smooth. Add praline mixture to the cooling ganache and then fold in the pistachios. Allow to cool for 1 to 2 hours.

Step 8.   Line a baking pan with a sheet of parchment paper. Using a small (1½-oz.) ice cream scoop, shape the ganache into mounds and place them on the parchment. Place in the refrigerator

Step 9. Dust you hands with powdered sugar, to keep them from sticking to the ganache. Shape each mound by hand into uniformly-shaped balls. Return truffles to a cool area while preparing the chocolate.

Step 10. To cover truffles, melt the chocolate in the top of a double boiler (105° to 110°F) or over a *bain-marie*. Thicken the chocolate with about ⅛ cup of the prepared simple syrup.

Step 11. Arrange two sheets of parchment paper on the work surface and have a fork nearby. Drop a truffle into the melted chocolate and retrieve by lifting out with the fork. Tap the covered truffle 4 or 5 times against the surface of the chocolate. The "surface tension" that results when both surfaces touch each other causes most of the excess chocolate to fall back into the pan.

Step 12. Scrape the side of the pan with the fork and then drag the fork (with the truffle on it) across one of the sheets of parchment. This helps remove the last of the excess chocolate. Place truffle on the clean sheet of parchment and allow to set. Repeat with remaining truffles.

Yield: 50 truffles

ACADEMY DARK
CHOCOLATE TRUFFLES

2¾ pounds bittersweet chocolate

2 cups heavy cream

2 ounces orange-flavored liqueur (Grand Marnier)

2 ounces almond-flavored liqueur (Amaretto)

1 teaspoon vanilla extract

6 ounces unsalted butter, soft

¼ cup unsweetened cocoa powder

Parchment paper

1 pound dark baker's chocolate
Melted white chocolate (optional)

Step 1.   Place the block of chocolate on a cutting board. Starting at one corner of the chocolate block and using the blade of a chef's knife like a paper cutter, shave down through the chocolate, cutting off small pieces at a time. As you shave each corner, rotate the block of chocolate in order to work on another corner. Continue shaving until all the chocolate is in small, similar-sized pieces. Set aside.

Step 2.   Pour the cream into a heavy, 3-quart saucepan. Add the orange liqueur, almond liqueur and vanilla. Place over moderate heat until cream begins to scald or reaches 180° to 190°F.

Step 3.   Remove from heat. Add the chocolate pieces and whisk for 2 to 3 minutes or until the chocolate sauce is satiny, smooth and homogenous. You should see no whisps of unincorporated cream or any lumps of chocolate remaining. This mixture is now called a *ganache*. Transfer the ganache to a bowl and cool. (Do not refrigerate or place on ice.)

Step 4.   When the temperature of the ganache has cooled below 90°F and feels slightly cool to the touch, cut the butter into small pieces and drop them, one at a time, into the ganache while stirring to incorporate. Allow to cool and become somewhat firm. (Note: If you add the butter before the ganache is below 90°F, the ganache will become grainy when it cools.)

Step 5.   Line a baking pan with a sheet of parchment paper. Using a small (1½-oz.) ice cream scoop, shape the ganache into mounds and place them on the parchment. Place in the refrigerator or a cool area and allow to set.

Step 6.   To keep the ganache from sticking to your hands, dust them with cocoa powder. Shape each mound by hand into uniformly-shaped balls. Return truffles to a cool area while preparing the chocolate.

Step 7.   To cover truffles, melt the chocolate in the top of a double boiler or over a *bain-marie*. Arrange two sheets of parchment paper on the work surface and have a fork nearby.

Step 8. Drop a truffle into the melted chocolate and retrieve by lifting out with the fork. Tap the covered truffle 4 or 5 times against the surface of the chocolate. The "surface tension" that results, when both surfaces touch each other, causes most of the excess chocolate to fall back into the pan.

Step 9. Scrape the side of the pan with the fork and then drag the fork (with the truffle on it) across one of the sheets of parchment. This helps remove the last of the excess chocolate. Place truffle on the clean sheet of parchment and allow to set. Repeat with remaining truffles.

Step 10. To decorate truffles, pour the melted white chocolate into a paper *cornet* and cut off a tiny corner of the tip. (You can also use a plastic squeeze bottle with a fine tip.) Pipe a decoration such as a spiral, starting from the outside and working in, or a cross-stitch pattern to decorate the top of each truffle.

Yield: 40 truffles.

VARIATION

Textured Truffles: Prepare truffles through Step 7 as directed above. Add **2 to 4 tablespoons Simple Syrup** (page 166) to the melted coating chocolate, stirring continuously until the chocolate becomes glossy and thickens. Coat your hands with some melted chocolate and then roll a truffle in your hands until well coated. Repeat with remaining truffles, adding more chocolate to your hands as needed.
Yield: 40 truffles

ACADEMY ALMOND
TOFFEE BARS

Parchment paper
Vegetable oil

½ cup ground almonds
4 cups granulated sugar
⅓ cup light corn syrup

1 cup water
1 pound unsalted butter
1 teaspoon salt
1 teaspoon vanilla extract
2 cups light baker's chocolate

Step 1. Line the inside of a 12 by 16-inch cookie sheet (with sides) with a sheet of parchment paper. Brush the parchment generously with oil and set aside. (An alternative to using a paper-lined cookie sheet would be *perimeter bars*. For infomation, see page 26.)

Step 2. To prepare syrup, combine the water, sugar and corn syrup in a heavy, 3-quart saucepan over moderate heat. Bring to a boil. This next procedure is very important. You want to prevent sugar crystals from forming on the inside of the pan, which would render it useless for glazing fruit. As the temperature of the syrup rises, use a pastry brush and some water to brush down the sides of the pan. (This is the exposed pan just above the surface of the boiling syrup.)

Step 3. Continue to boil, brushing the sides continuously, until the temperature of the syrup reaches 280°F on the candy thermometer (called the *soft-crack stage*). You can test for the soft-crack stage by placing a drop of the boiling sugar-syrup into cold water. It should form firm, pliable threads when immersed.

Step 4. Cut the butter into pieces and slowly drop them, one at a time, into the foaming syrup while stirring constantly. Continue to cook until syrup turns light caramel in color and reaches 315°F on a candy thermometer.

Step 5. Add salt and continue to cook, stirring constantly, until syrup turns medium caramel in color and reaches 320°F.

Step 6. Stir in almond meal, just until incorporated, and remove from heat immediately.

Step 7. Quickly stir in vanilla. Then pour *immediately* onto the prepared pan, taking care that the liquid mixture does not overflow the pan. Set aside for 5 to 10 minutes or until toffee starts to firm but is still soft to the touch.

Step 8. Using a well-oiled knife, score through the entire pan of toffee, cutting it into pieces approximately ½-inch wide by 3 inches long. Set aside to cool completely.

Step 9.   Break toffee along the score lines into bars. If any of the bars shatter or break into pieces, keep them to use as ice cream toppings.

Step 10.   Meanwhile, melt the chocolate in the top of a double boiler or over a *bain-marie*. Arrange two sheets of parchment paper on the work surface and have a fork nearby.

Step 11.   Using a dinner fork, dip the toffee bars, one at a time, into the melted chocolate. Lift out with the fork, scrape the fork against the side of the pan. Drag the fork (with the toffee bar on it) across one of the sheets of parchment. This helps remove the last of the excess chocolate. Place toffee bar on the clean sheet of parchment and allow to set. Repeat with remaining bars.

Yield: 35 bars

POSTSCRIPTS

NUTRITION

	Calories	Protein (gm.)	Carbohydrates (gm.)	Saturated Fats (gm.)	Cholesterol (mg.)	Sodium (mg.)
Academy Dark Truffle	284	3.3	21.7	24.2	16	6
Academy Light Truffle	329	2.0	37.3	20.8	19	23
Academy Toffee Bars	256	.08	31	15.3	0	70
Ancho Chile Beef	277	24.6	5.9	17.2	70	82
Baked Salmon Terrine	310	12.6	6.2	26.3	144	542
Banana Fritters	533	7.1	80.5	34.7	72	122
Basic Béchamel Sauce	5	.02	.09	.02	0	3
Basic Brown Sauce	61	.08	4.6	4.6	12	60
Basic Chicken Stock	21	0.5	2.3	1.2	0	5
Basic Egg Pasta	450	17.7	75.2	7.5	229	265
Basic Fish Stock	42	.06	3.1	3.2	5	27
Basic Tomato Sauce	18	0.4	3.2	0.7	1	68
Basic Vegetable Stock	15	0	0.1	0.9	0	4
Basic Velouté Sauce	38	1.2	2.9	2.5	8.2	30
Beef Stock	25	.09	2.5	1.7	1	6
Bercy Sauce	74	1.0	6.1	4.8	12	63
Béarnaise Sauce	176	1.3	0.1	19.2	128	178
Black Bean Sausage	252	22	26.6	6.1	0	327
Black Pepper Tagliatelle	486	15.1	63	19.5	171	371
Bordelaise Sauce	85	1.0	5.8	6.3	16	68
Bouquet Salad	587	12	42.9	44.3	152	291
Braised Chicken Portuguese	605	66.3	13.9	28.4	183	561
Buttermilk Chicken	858	48.7	58.3	46.8	163	1284
Carrot Terrine	914	32.1	20.2	81	130	382
Champagne Sorbet	335	3.6	336	12.5	76.8	48
Cheesecake Soufflé	210	4.1	33.5	7.1	21	99
Chestnut & Carrot Soup	964	10.5	88.5	67	189	168
Chicken & Apple Sausage	229	37.9	7.8	44.1	112	422
Chicken Ballotine	330	31	12.5	18.2	103	772
Chicken Dijon	507	30.3	11.1	38.1	149	438

NUTRITION

	Calories	Protein (gm.)	Carbohydrates (gm.)	Saturated Fats (gm.)	Cholesterol (mg.)	Sodium (mg.)
Chicken Madras	780	35.5	40.9	54.6	112	249
Chicken Paprikash	963	70.6	107	31.2	211	1042
Chinese Steamed Fish	313	33.7	8	16	82	443
Chocolate Mocha Cake	942	13.8	101.5	56.3	266	524
Chocolate Bread Pudding	922	99.4	77.2	35.7	154	583
Corn & Clam Fritters	259	4.3	13.7	20.8	41	543
Country-style Pâté	1025	55.5	35.4	73.4	444	1731
Creole Sauce	36	0.4	2.9	2.5	1	71
Curry Sauce	52	3.6	2.2	5.9	17	42
Demi-glace	66	0.9	5.4	4.8	12	62
Deviled Crab Cakes	766	24.8	11.5	65.5	131	1055
Five Pea Soup	657	28.2	82.5	25.6	9	411
Four Onion Soup	240	4.9	19.4	17.1	30	48
Fresh Fruit Tart	511	4.8	85.4	17.8	65	188
Frozen Cherry Soufflé	283	4.3	39	11.7	41	46
Frozen Watermelon Bombe	353	4.6	56.9	13.2	40	166
Gingered Prawns & Noodles	840	37.3	81.2	42.7	221	1314
Glaced Fruit	197	1.6	78.3	11.6	8	3
Grilled California Halibut	747	55.6	23.3	46.9	118	173
Grilled Chicken with Marsala	583	32	232	41.4	104	327
Grilled Corn Chowder	791	15.9	67.4	54.1	120	372
Grilled Flank Steak	858	47.1	69.2	39.9	159	187
Grilled Moroccan Chicken	368	33.5	50.7	2.2	67	486
Grilled Polynesian Shrimp	154	12.9	23.9	1.7	109	129
Grilled Prawns with Quinoa	268	14.1	38.5	2.1	126	108
Grilled Teriyaki Beef	233	27.7	7.9	8.9	79	384
Grilled Tuscan Chicken	514	35.7	61.6	14.5	89.1	667
Grilled Vegetable Gazpacho	353	5.4	30.8	25.5	0	577
Hollandaise Sauce	176	1.3	0.1	19.2	128	178
Hungarian Sauce	35	0.3	1.8	3.1	8	30

NUTRITION

	Calories	Protein (gm.)	Carbohydrates (gm.)	Saturated Fats (gm.)	Cholesterol (mg.)	Sodium (mg.)
Individual Baked Alaska	526	8.3	10.8	11	307	208
Lemon Dill Pasta	439	16.7	76.8	6.5	184	254
Madeira Sauce	88	.05	2.8	2.1	1	39
Marinated Calamari Salad	506	14.9	3.3	48.9	182	156
Mendocino Poached Pears	541	1.2	112	3.2	0	11
Mushroom Sauce	84	1.1	5.9	6.3	16	77
Orange Buttermilk Ice Cream	199	3.9	34	1.1	5	129
Oxtail Consommé	330	32.2	7.5	78.1	159	150
Poached Beef Tenderloin	474	39.4	23.5	26.1	227	220
Poached Whole Salmon	493	56.9	10	22.4	173	147
Pork Tenderloin	1002	52.8	101	46.2	157	498
Portuguese Sauce	30	0.3	3.3	1.6	1	69
Pork Adobo	371	272	31.4	14.2	108	488
Sauerbraten with Cabbage	842	35.1	36	92.4	156	769
Sautéed Beef Lemon Grass	172	19.5	7.4	7.0	52	641
Sautéed Snapper Franciscan	457	40	28.1	17.1	64	338
Sautéed Snapper Galician	404	37.3	14.2	19.5	63	331
Seabass en Papillote	586	15.1	37.4	44.2	132	490
Seafood Sausage	467	48.3	12.5	24.7	200	738
Shredded Chicken	299	20.9	23.7	13.2	45	584
Sonoma Kiev	1116	71.5	64.1	64.1	469	891
Spanish Sauce	38	0.5	3.1	2.5	1	68
Spinach Fettucine Alfredo	659	27.6	79.4	25.1	203	1060
Spinach Pasta	435	16.2	78.1	5.8	147	481
Strawberry Sherbet	213	1.9	33	10.5	8	19
Suprême Sauce	39	1.3	3.1	2.5	8.2	30
Tri-color Shrimp Ravioli	797	44.5	84.7	21.5	418	1261
Turkey Pâté	221	13.7	5.9	16	64	453
Whole Wheat Pappardelle	785	36.1	82.8	35.4	246	1469
Whole Wheat Pasta	411	18.1	72.6	6.6	163	247

INDEX

INDEX

INDEX

INDEX

INDEX

INDEX

INDEX

Terrine, baked salmon & scallop, 61
Terrine, carrot, cauliflower & broccoli, 62
Timbales, herbed cheese custard, 58
Toffee almond bars, Academy, 170
Tomato sauce, basic, 40
Tomato relish, 114
Tomato-cilantro relish, 128
Tri-color Bay shrimp ravioli with
    white clam sauce, 82
Truffled banana fritters with kiwi
    & tangerine coulis, 158
Truffles, dark chocolate, 168
Truffles, light, 166
Tuiles, almond, 160
Tulip cookie cups, 138
Turkey pâté with cranberry sauce, 66
Tuscan chicken, grilled, 112

V

Vegetable gazpacho, grilled, 47
Vegetable stock, basic, 30
Vegetable terrine with carrot & mushroom
    garnish, 63

Vegetables, marinated, 64
Vegetables, steamed baby, 122
Velouté sauce, basic, 36
Verte, sauce, 62
Vinaigrette, caviar, 60

W

Watermelon bombe, frozen, 145
Wheat pasta, whole, 79
White clam sauce, 82
Whole wheat pappardelle with peas &
    andouille sausage, 84
Whole wheat pasta, 79
Wild mushroom Marsala sauce, 114
Wild mushroom sauté, 126

Z

Zest, 28
Zester, 28

(*Italicized* words are found in the glossary.)

CALIFORNIA CULINARY ACADEMY

The California Culinary Academy was founded in San Francisco in 1977 as a professional school for chef training. Unique among chef training schools, the Academy is situated near the heart of downtown San Francisco, a city internationally acclaimed for its world-class dining establishments. With more than three thousand restaurants, the city provides employment and learning opportunities for students at the Academy. One of the first such schools in the western United States, the Academy is now recognized as a leader and innovator in the Culinary Arts. The Academy's proximity to several wine-producing regions is unparalleled among American culinary schools. Courses, special tastings, field trips and food and wine pairing contests for students focus on this unique opportunity.

The Academy has nine professional kitchens for practical training including a pastry shop, bakery, candy kitchen, garde manger, butchery, three production kitchens and a fully-equipped demonstration kitchen, as well as three classrooms. Additional learning facilities include three student-staffed restaurants open to the general public for lunch and dinner five days per week and a retail shop for the sale of products made by students. The Academy has an instructional staff of 17 chef instructors, four maître d'hotel instructors, and six restaurant and kitchen management instructors. The Academy's Educational Advisory Committee includes Julia Child, Robert Mondavi, Jeremiah Tower, Martin Yan, Richard Swig, Bert Cutino, Hubert Keller and André Fournier. The objective of the California Culinary Academy is to train suitable individuals for entry level positions or advancement as a cook, chef or baker in the foodservice industry. The Academy is accredited by the National Association of Trade and Technical Schools and the American Culinary Federation Educational Institute Accrediting Commission. Upon graduation students are able to develop careers in cooking, dining room service, restaurant management and ownership. Students are admitted six times per year: January, February, April, June, September and October. Admission is competitive and open to those who have a high school diploma or equivalency certificate.

Curriculum

The Academy offers a curriculum of 2,035 hours focusing on the fundamentals of modern classical cooking and baking. The curriculum includes 23 hands-on instruction laboratory classes which are taught over 51 weeks and 12 food and beverage management lecture-style classes taught over 13 weeks. The professional curriculum covers every aspect of food preparation beginning with knife skills and advancing through stocks, soups, sauces, mousses, salads, vegetables, seafood, poultry, meats, breads and desserts providing students with a complete understanding of the intricacies of professional cooking. Special weekend and evening cooking and restaurant management classes are offered by the Academy. Students, professionals in the foodservice industry and the general public are invited to attend these classes. Special courses for large groups may be custom-designed.

(over)

For more information . . .

For information or to arrange an appointment to visit the Academy, call us at 1-800-BAY-CHEF (1-800-229-2433) or 415-771-3536 if you live within the San Francisco Bay Area, or please return this reply card.

Name _____
      Last   First

Phone   (   )

Address _____

City _____ State ____ Zip ____

High School Graduation Date _____

Please check your preference:

❏ Please call me to arrange a visit to the campus

❏ Please arrange to have a representative contact me

The best time to call is: _____

Program of interest:

❏ 16-month program   ❏ Continuing Education

For a friend . . .

Please send a copy of the Admissions Bulletin to a friend who is interested in the programs of study at the California Culinary Academy:

Name _____
      Last   First

Phone   (   )

Address _____

City _____ State ____ Zip ____

Program of interest:

❏ 16-month program   ❏ Continuing Education

CALIFORNIA CULINARY ACADEMY

The Profession

The foodservice industry is one of the fastest growing industries in the United States. The Bureau of Labor Statistics projects an increase in demand of at least 50 percent through the 1990s for restaurant chefs and cooks. This growth will provide more than 200,000 career opportunities in our dynamic field. Graduates of the Academy have been especially successful in developing careers based on their specific areas of interset in the Culinary Arts. A majority of our graduates are placed directly into foodservice positions after graduation and most are still employed in the foodservice industry.

Whether your goal is to work in a traditional American or European restaurant, open your own restaurant or catering business, broaden your culinary knowledge or perfect your cooking technique, the California Culinary Academy can help you. For most aspiring chefs in America, the dream of studying in the classrooms and kitchens of Europe and Asia is out of reach. At the California Culinary Academy we are dedicated to making that educational experience available to you.

Visiting the Academy

Admissions Office Visits and Tours: You are encouraged to visit the California Culinary Academy to meet our admissions representatives and tour the Academy's facilities. Admissions representatives are available to talk to you and your family Monday through Friday from 8:00 a.m. to 5:00 p.m. Note: Group presentations and tours of Academy facilities are conducted Monday through Friday at 3:00 p.m. Personal tours and interviews are available by appointment at other times. Appointments are recommended for all Academy visits. Please plan to spend approximately 1½ to 2 hours for your visit to the California Culinary Academy.

Telephone toll-free from outside San Francisco: 1-800-BAY-CHEF (1-800-229-2433)
Telephone from within the San Francisco Bay Area: 415-771-3536 • Fax Number: 415-771-2108

Restaurant Patrons: Visitors to the California Culinary Academy may dine in one of the Academy's three restaurants: The Academy Grill, The Carême Room and Cyril's. When making reservations, identify yourself as an "Admissions Office Visitor" to the Academy. All Admissions Visitors are provided with a discount coupon which may be used for lunch or dinner at any of the Academy's restaurants. The Academy Grill, The Carême Room and Cyril's are all training facilities for our students. We hope you enjoy visiting our center for culinary education and we appreciate your interest in the California Culinary Academy.

For more information about the California Culinary Academy please fill out the form(s) on the reverse side and mail to:
**California Culinary Academy,
Admissions
625 Polk Street
San Francisco, CA 94102**

or call **415-771-3536**
(or **1-800-BAY-CHEF** from outside San Francisco).

For more information about the California Culinary Academy please fill out the form(s) on the reverse side and mail to:
**California Culinary Academy,
Admissions
625 Polk Street
San Francisco, CA 94102**

or call **415-771-3536**
(or **1-800-BAY-CHEF** from outside San Francisco).